SHAI
Ever

Welcome to Shanghai!

This opening fold-out contains a general map of Shanghai to help you visualise the six large districts explored in this guide, plus a wealth of practical information, handy tips and detailed maps to enable you to get the swing of the city.

Discover Shanghai through six districts and six maps

A Bund (Waitan) / Nanjing Donglu
B Renmin Guangchang / Nanjing Xilu / Zhabei
C Old Town (Nanshi)
D Huaihai Lu / Fuxing Lu / Xujiahui
E Hongkou
F Pudong

For each district there is a double-page of addresses (restaurants – listed in ascending order of price – cafés, bars, music venues and shops), followed by a fold-out map for the relevant area with the essential places to see (indicated on the map by a star ★). These places are by no means all that Shanghai has to offer, but to us they are unmissable. The grid-referencing system (**A** B2) makes it easy for you to pinpoint addresses quickly on the map.

Transport and hotels in Shanghai

The last fold-out consists of a transport map and four pages of practical information that include a selection of hotels.

Index

Lists all the street names, sites and addresses featured in this guide.

KEY DATES

12th-15th c. The Huangpu River's resources help to create a settlement.
1842 Shanghai, by now a port and weaving center, is opened up to international trade by the Treaty of Nanjing.
1921 Creation of the Chinese Communist Party; half of the country's workers live in the city.
1949 Proclamation of the People's Republic. Shanghai, considered a symbol of capitalism, is neglected until 1976.
1990 Development of Pudong. Shanghai becomes the showcase of 'market Socialism'.

PUDONG AND THE PEARL TV TOWER

ARCHITECTURE

There are a few significan examples of Chinese classical architecture. **Huxinting Tea House** (**C** B2), **Yu Garden** (**C** B1); **Longhua Temple** (2853 Longhua Lu, off map, sout of the city) is the city's oldest Buddhist temple (15th c.). Octagonal pagoda dating from the Song dynasty (960–1279).
Legacy of the concessions
The concessions rented to Westerners between 1842 and 1943 used a variety of styles – Art Deco, neoclassical, etc.
Shikumen architecture
Also referred to as *lilongs*, these collective housing units offered a hybrid between the British row house and the Chinese courtyard house. Built in the concessions between 1860 and 1939 as lodgings for Chinese families, the terraced houses and their inner courtyards were linked by a network of alleyways. Each had a large gate (*shikumen* means 'stone gate') which was closed at night. Today many *shikumen* are being demolished and replaced by commercial developments.
Shanxi nanlu (**D** D2-3); **Xintiandi district** (**D** E-F2)

MODERN SHANGHAI

World Financial Center (**F** B2) It was going to be the world's highest building (1,575 ft) but is already ranking second after Taipei's 101 building (1,670 feet). Completion of works end 2007.

Tel. 6433 6880 (after hours emergencies 6433 3936)
www.usembassy-china.org.cn
International Post Office (**E** B4)
→ *250 Beisuzhou Lu*
Tel. 6325 2070
Daily 730am–10pm
Shanghai N°1 Pharmacy (**A** C3)
→ *616 Nanjing Donglu*
Tel. 6322 4567
Daily 9am–10pm
The biggest pharmacy in town; imported medicines.

PINYIN

The official transcription of Chinese in Roman letters.
Pronunciation
'c' = ts, 'ch' = tch, 'r' = j, 'q' = ch, 'x' = s, 'z' = dz, 'zh' = dj, 'a' = ah, 'e' = er, 'h' = guttural h

GETTING AROUND

The most important roads (*lu*) are divided into sections:
central (*zhong*), north (*bei*), south (*nan*), east (*dong*) and west (*xi*); 1st (*yi*) and 2nd (*er*). Thus Beijing Xilu is the western part of Beijing road.
Large axes
The inner ring road (29 miles) was opened in 1994. Two freeways cross the city center on over-passes: one running north-south, the other east-west (to the Bund). They cross near the People's Square, the city's geographical center.

ENGLISH-LANGUAGE MAGAZINES

Free monthly publications distributed in hotels, shops, bars and tourist sights.
That's Shanghai
→ *www.thatsmagazine.com*
Shanghai's answer to *Time Out*. A reference for addresses and cultural activities.
Metrozine
Bilingual (English-Chinese).

Plenty of information and practical addresses.
Shanghai Talk
Extensive lists of addresses with commentaries.
Shanghai Voyage
Suggestions for excursions and articles on the city.

OPENING HOURS

Banks and official offices
→ *Mon-Fri 8am–5pm*
Stores
→ *Generally daily 10am–7pm (10pm on Nanjing Donglu)*
Restaurants
→ *Generally daily 11am– 10pm (non-stop service)*
Hairdressers
→ *Daily 10am–midnight*
Haircuts at any time, with a massage as a bonus.

DIARY OF EVENTS

Public holidays
→ *Jan 1; May 1; Oct 1; and Chinese New Year*

CITY PROFILE

- Municipality covering 2,400 sq. miles, governed directly by the State
- 14 million inhabitants
- China's main port and the fourth largest in the world ■ GDP/ inhabitant (US$5,000) five times higher than national average ■ Growth: 11% per year since 1993
- More than 5,000 tower blocks were built since 1990 ■ When it's noon in Shanghai it's 11pm in New York (day before), and 4am in London (same day)
- Currency: (¥) the yuan £1 = ¥13.50; $1 = ¥7.75 ¥100 = $12.90 /£7.30

MORNING EXERCISE ON THE BUND

INTERNET

Websites

→ www.cnto.org
Official site of China's National Tourist Office in the USA.

→ www.shanghaitour.net
Shanghai's Tourist Office.

→ www.shanghai-ed.com
Bars, restaurants, places to visit; cultural and sporting events.

→ www.sh.com
Search engine (leisure, health and shopping).

→ www.shanghaiexpat.com
Full of interesting tips whether you're an expat or not.

Internet café

Trying to connect to the Internet in a hotel should be simple (dial 8888 from a simple phone plug) but in reality it often proves to be a frustrating experience. It might be best to sign up for a free webmail account (Hotmail, Gmail, etc.) and access it in an Internet café.
Shanghai Library (D B2)
→ 1555 Huaihai Zhonglu
Tel. 6445 5555
Daily 9am–8.30pm
A large Internet café popular with students. Reasonable prices.

FORMALITIES

You need a visa and passport valid six months after your planned return from Shanghai. It takes two weeks to obtain a visa.

Chinese embassies

In London
31 Portland Place
Tel. 020 7631 1430 (2–4pm, consulate); http://china.embassyhomepage.com
→ 100 West Erie St
Tel. (312) 803 0097/8 (8am–noon); www.chinaconsulatechicago.org
In New York
→ 520 12th Ave, New York,

NY 10036. Tel. (212) 868 207 (2–4.30pm consulate) www. nyconsulate.prchina. org/eng

TOURIST INFO

Tourist Hotline

→ Tel. 962 020
Daily, 24 hrs (in English)
Usual tourist information.
Jingan District Tourist Information & Service Center (B C4)
→ 1699 Nanjing Xilu
Tel. 6248 3259
Municipal tourist office.
Travel Professionals Shanghai (off **D** A4)
→ 822 Yishan Lu
Tel. 6485 2218
They can organize your stay, excursions and the hiring of English-speaking guides.

TELEPHONE

Shanghai to rest of China
→ 0 + city code (10 for

Beijing) + number
USA / UK to Shanghai
→ 011 (from the US)/ 00 (from the UK) + 86 (China) + 21 (Shanghai) + number
Shanghai to the USA/UK
→ 00 + 1 (US)/44 (UK) + number (without initial 0 for the UK)

Useful numbers

Information
→ 114
Police
→ 110
Fire department
→ 190
Hua Shan Hospital
Foreign Expatriate
Dispensary (**D** B1)
→ 12 Wulumuqi Zhonglu
Tel. 6248 5085

USEFUL ADDRESSES

UK Consulate (B D4)
→ Room 301, Shanghai Center, 1376 Nanjing Xilu
Tel. 6279 7650
US Consulate (B D4)
→ 1469 Huaihai Zhonglu

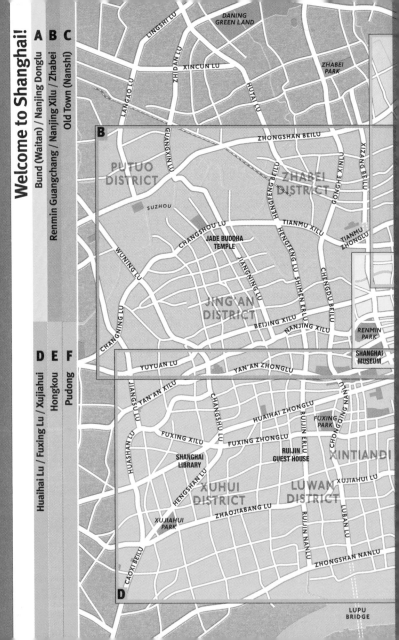

Welcome to Shanghai!

A Bund (Waitan) / Nanjing Donglu
B Renmin Guangchang / Nanjing Xilu / Zhabei
C Old Town (Nanshi)

D Huaihai Lu / Fuxing Lu / Xujiahui
E Hongkou
F Pudong

DANING GREEN LAND

LINGSHI LU
XINCUN LU
ZHIDAN LU
LANGAO LU
HUTAI LU
ZHABEI PARK

B

PUTUO DISTRICT
GUANGXIN LU
ZHONGSHAN BEILU
HENGFENG BEILU
ZHABEI DISTRICT
XIZANG BEILU
XINLU
GONGHE XINLU

SUZHOU
CHANGSHOU LU
TIANMU XILU
TIANMU ZHONGLU
TIANMU PARK

JADE BUDDHA TEMPLE
HENGFENG LU
SHIMEN ERLU
CHENGDU BEILU

WUNING LU
JIANGNING LU

JING'AN DISTRICT
BEIJING XILU
NANJING XILU
RENMIN PARK

CHANGNING LU
SHANGHAI MUSEUM

D

YUYUAN LU
YAN'AN ZHONGLU

JIANGSU LU
YAN'AN XILU
CHANGSHU LU
HUAIHAI ZHONGLU
RUIJIN YILU
FUXING PARK
CHONGQING NANLU

FUXING XILU
FUXING ZHONGLU
RUIJIN GUEST HOUSE
XINTIANDI

HUASHAN LU
SHANGHAI LIBRARY
HENGSHAN LU
XUHUI DISTRICT
LUWAN DISTRICT
XUJIAHUI LU

XUJIAHUI PARK
ZHAOJIABANG LU
RUIJIN NANLU
LUBAN LU

CAOXI BEILU
ZHONGSHAN NANLU

LUPU BRIDGE

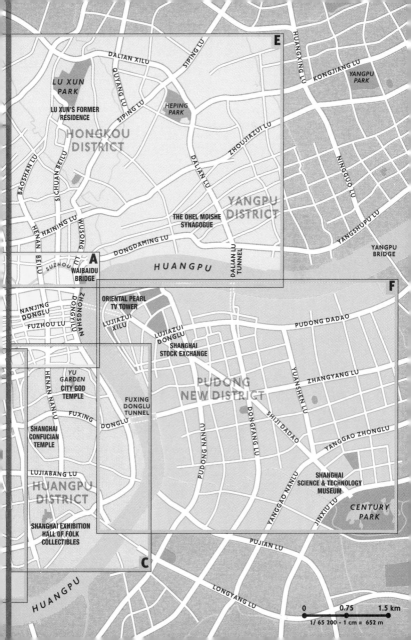

EXCURSIONS FROM SHANGHAI

Province:

JIANGSU Name

Frontier

EXCURSIONS

Escape to the lush countryside of Jiangnan, literally 'south of the river' (Yangzi), by going just a few stops on the subway or traveling for under an hour by train.

Shanghai Botanical Garden

→ *1111 Longwu Lu (subway to Shanghai South Railway Station) Tel. 5436 3369 Daily 7.30am–4.30pm*

A 200-acre park, famous throughout the country for its remarkable collection of bonsais (9,000 specimens).

Shanghai Guyi Garden (Nanxiang)

→ *218 Huyi Lu (bus to Shanghai Sightseeing Bus Center, line 6A) Tel. 5912 1535 Daily 6am–5.30pm*

The Garden of Ancient Splendors, laid out in the 16th century by Zhu Sansong, a sculptor of bamboo.

Zhouzhuang and Tongli

→ *Bus from Shanghai Sightseeing Bus Center, line 2*

These two villages crisscrossed by canals near Lake Dianshan were founded many centuries ago. Opulent Ming houses (1368–1644).

Suzhou

→ *Train from Shanghai Railway Station every 30 mins (journey: 40 mins to 1 hr)*

This 'Venice of the East' boasts some magnificent and very old gardens. Do not miss the garden of the Master of the Nets (12th century).

Jiuliang yanzi: local dessert made with rice pastry, eaten at New Year.

Xiaolong bao: steamed ravioli filled with pork or shrimps.

Tipping

Do not tip – it could cause offence.

SHOPPING

Department stores

Main streets like Nanjing Lu, Huaihai Lu and Sichuan Beilu are packed with stores.

Maison Mode (D C2)

→ *1312 Huaihai Zhonglu Tel. 6431 0100 Daily 10am–9.30pm*

Department store within a beautiful Art Deco building, selling clothes from all the major fashion labels.

Shanghai Center (B CD4)

→ *1376 Nanjing Xilu Tel. 6279 8600*

Hotel, medical center, stores and bars.

ENTERTAINMENT

Movies

The Chinese movie industry is coming to life again with large-scale productions; program in the free magazine *Quo*.

Guotai (D D1)

→ *870 Huaihai Zhonglu Tel. 5404 2095*

Movie theater that first opened its doors in 1932. Chinese and foreign films.

Shanghai Film Art Center (off map)

→ *160 Xinhua Lu Tel. 6280 6088*

Shanghai Film festival in September.

Theater

Shanghai Grand Theater (B F4)

→ *300 Renmin dadao Reservation box office Tel. 6386 8686 Daily 9am–7.30pm*

Lyceum Theater (D D2)

→ *57 Maoming Nanlu Tel. 6217 8530 (bookings)*

Music

Shanghai Concert Hall (B F4)

→ *523 Yan'an Donglu Tel. 5386 6666*

Classical music concerts.

Circus

Shanghai Center Theater (B CD4)

→ *1376 Nanjing Xilu Tel. 6279 8614*

Acrobatic shows every night at 7.30pm.

Shanghai Circus Center (off map)

→ *2266 Gonghe Xinlu Tel. 5665 6622*

The circus center, north of the city.

Nightlife

Bars concentrated on Hengshan Lu and below Maoming Nanlu.

Xintiandi (D F1)

→ *Taicang Lu*

Stores, restaurants and bars spread over 130 acres in this 'new world', an area that has recently become fashionable.

ANGHAI BY NIGHT

en night falls, the
eets light up in a
ze of neon.

nks of the Huangpu
the west bank, old
ldings with illuminated
ades and gigantic
ninous billboards.
the east, glittering
dern tower blocks.

d town
btle lighting on the
eastern-wing roofs on
yuan Lu (**C** B2).

aihai Zhonglu
particularly brightly
corated avenue.

ople's Square
e Opera House and
useums are dramatically
minated.

NANJING DONGLU AT NIGHT

TOWER BLOCKS IN PUDONG

e traditional holidays
ow the lunar calendar.

nuary–February
nese New Year
→ *First three days of first
ar month*
e biggest holiday of the
ar. The locals spruce up
eir houses and let off
ecrackers in the street.

ntern Festival
→ *15th day of first lunar month*
ht up the area around
e Yu Garden for the first
l moon of the year.

arch–April
stival of the Dead
→ *April 4 or 5*
e Chinese clean the
mbs of their ancestors and
ake offerings to them in
e temples.

anghai International
ower Festival
→ *Odd-numbered years,
rly April*
llions of exotic
wers are on display in
angfeng Park.

Longhua Temple Fair
→ *Middle of third lunar
month*
This 300-year-old fair in
the grounds of the
Longhua Temple presents
craftwork and Buddhist
ceremonies.

**Shanghai International
Tea Culture Festival**
→ *For one week, from the
last Sat in April*
A celebration of tea in
front of the railway station:
tastings and ceremonies.

May–June
**Shanghai International
Cartoon Carnival**
→ *Early May*
Festival of cartoon movies,
video and computer games.

September–October
Confucius's birthday
→ *27th day of eighth lunar
month*

Tourism Fair
→ *October*
Artistic and gastronomic
presentations celebrating
the city's culture.

MUSEUMS

Opening hours
→ *Daily 9am–4.30pm*
The ticket office closes ½ hr
to 1hr before the museum.

Discounts
Combination ticket
→ *Transferable ticket with
two or three coupons, valid
for the Shanghai Museum,
Shanghai Grand Theater
and/or Shanghai Urban
Planning Exhibition Hall*
Discount for admission to
the three cultural centers in
the People's Square (or to
two of your choice).

EATING OUT

Chinese cooking
China boasts four main
'schools' of gastronomy: that
of Beijing and Shandong,
with a preference for strong
flavors (garlic, onion,
vinegar); that of Sichuan,
which is very spicy; that of
Shanghai and the lower

Yangzi, based on fish,
with sweet and sour flavors;
and, finally, that of Canton
and Shaozhou, which
corresponds to most
Europeans' idea of
'Chinese food'.

Eating habits
Three complete meals a day.
Breakfast consists of cooked
pork meats and congee
sprinkled with pieces of
pork. Lunch and dinner
traditionally comprises a
bowl of rice or noodles,
accompanied by plates of
meat and/or fish. In
Shanghai the locals often
eat at stands in the street.

Short glossary
Baozi: small loaf cooked
with steam.
Congee: rice porridge
popular in southern China.
Dim sum: small steamed
dishes, literally meaning
'going straight to the heart'
in Cantonese.
Huoguo: spicy hotpot, very
popular in winter.

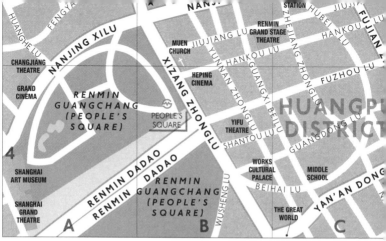

CUSTOM HOUSE

SHANGHAI PUDONG DEVELOPMENT BANK

BUND MUSEUM

★ Industrial & Commercial Bank of China (A E2)

→ 24 Zhongshan Dongyilu
The impressive façade juxtaposes two Ionic pillars with China's national flag (red with a cluster of yellow stars). The building was designed in 1924 by the Palmer & Turner architectural firm to house a branch of the Bank of Yokohama. Its opulent past is still evident in the long entrance hall: marble floors with geometric motifs, coffered ceilings and gold-tinted skylight.

★ Bank of China (A E2)

→ 23 Zhongshan Dongyilu

This skyscraper (Palmer & Turner and Lu Qianshou, 1937) combines Western forms and materials (reinforced concrete) with traditional Chinese decorative devices (curved roof). Of the 33 floors originally planned, only 16 were finally built, in order not to overshadow the Peace Hotel.

★ Peace Hotel (A E2)

→ 19a Zhongshan Dongyilu
www.shanghaipeacehotel.com
Originally called Cathay Hotel, the Peace Hotel was built by Palmer & Turner in 1929 on one of the city's prime sites, using the most advanced techniques of the

time to flaunt the power of the property developer Victor Sassoon. This British magnate, descended from Iraqi Jewish traders, made his home on the top floor, under the pyramidal roof. He spared no expense: replicas of lamps from the Great Synagogue in Damascus shine on the Italian marble in the foyer; Lalique glass works; the stained-glass windows on the stairs are inspired by Fernand Léger, while the ironwork draws on Art Deco.

★ Peace Hotel South, ex Palace Hotel (A E2)

→ 19 Zhongshan Dongyilu
This is one of the first luxury

hotels on the Bund (Scott & Carter, 1906), the only one built from brick. It has a pink and white façade, and a tou of baroque in the foye restaurant interiors.

★ Bank of Shanghai (A E3)

→ 14 Zhongshan Dongy
Although dwarfed by t Customs House next d this building at the en the Bund (1940) still impresses with its Art-lines projecting boldly to the sky. The lobby b an imposing staircase black and yellow grani as well as ramps made wrought iron.

SHANGHAI No. 1
DEPARTMENT STORE
上海市第一百货商店

SILK AND
SATIN STORE

POST
OFFICE

BEIJING XILU

GULING LU

GULING LU

BAIHE

TIANJIN LU

TIANJIN LU

NINGBO LU

GUIZHOU LU

LIANHE LU

ZHIFU LU

CHANGSHA LU

XINZHA LU

WUFU LONG

NINGBO LU

GUJIA LONG

ZHONGGUO
THEATRE

HUANGPU
THEATRE

BEIJING DONGLU

XIAMEN LU

TAXI
STATION

BEIJING

FUJIAN ZHONGLU

XIAMEN LU

ZHEJIANG ZHONGLU

XIZANG ZHONGLU

XIAMEN LU

SHANXI

NANSUZHOU LU

BEIJING XILU

BEISUZHOU LU

NANSUZHOU LU

NICHENG
QIAO

GUOQING LU

FUJIAN BEILU

BEISUZHOU LU

NANSUZHOU LU

SUZHOU

SHANXI BEILU

FUJIAN BEILU

TIANTONG LU

ZHEJIANG BEILU

QUFU LU

WEN AN LU

XIZANG BEILU

MIDDLE
SCHOOL

GANSU LU

KAIFENG LU

ZHEJIANG BEILU

QIPU LU

SHANXI BEILU

TANGOU LU

FUJIAN BEILU

TANGOU LU

QIPU LU

GANSU LU

QIPU LU

BEIZHAN
HOSPITAL

XINJIANG LU

REHE LU

OIPU LU

C

B

A

PEACE HOTEL

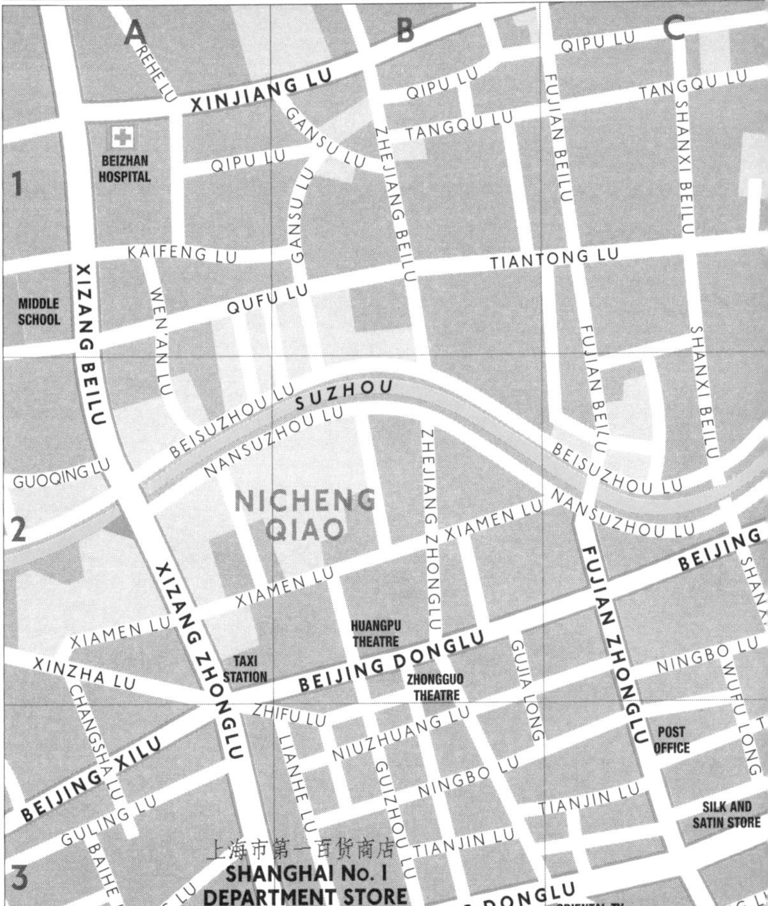

BANK OF CHINA

INDUSTRIAL & COMMERCIAL BANK OF CHINA

The curvaceous waterfront avenue of Zhongshan Dongyilu is famous in the East under it former name: the Bund, or Waitan for the Chinese. It is a magical place at dawn, when local people assemble on the promenade to practise tai chi and fly kites, while barges glide down the Huangpu. Later on in the day tourists flock to pose for photos in front of the famous buildings bordering the avenue, architectural showcase of the 'Paris of the East'. At nightfall these imposing relics of the thriving capitalism of the early 20th century are lit up, and Nanjing Donglu blossoms in a thousand fluorescent colors to advertise the virtues of the latest products to the potential buyers thronging the street.

LIUYUAN MIANGUAN   DRAGON PHOENIX DINING ROOM

RESTAURANTS

Liuyuan Mianguan
留缘面馆 (**A** E3)
→ 7 Sashi Yilu
Tel. 6321 4046
Daily 7am–9pm
Come here for the *xiaolong bao* (ravioli stuffed with pork and shrimps), which are then steamed in the bamboo baskets stacked up outside. One of the best places to enjoy this famous specialty in its full simplicity. Carte ¥10.

Dragon Phoenix Dining Room 龙凤厅 (**A** E2)
→ 20 Nanjing Donglu
Tel. 6321 6888 Daily
11.30am–2pm, 5.30–10pm
One of the restaurants in the Peace Hotel, with a particularly fine view of the boats going up and down the Huangpu. Dining room decorated with dragons, waitresses in *qipao* (figure-hugging dresses with slits up the sides), and Shanghai, Canton and Sichuan cuisine. Carte ¥140.

M on the Bund
米民西餐厅 (**A** F3)
→ 20 Guangdong Lu
Tel. 6350 9988 Tue-Sun
noon–2.30pm, 6–10.30pm
www.m-restaurantgroup.com
This restaurant's wonderful terrace overlooking the Bund is a favorite meeting place for English-speaking expatriates. Stylish design and adventurous culinary fusions, using extremely fresh ingredients. Good wine list. Lunch and brunch ¥200, dinner ¥500.

BARS

The Glamour Bar (**A** F3)
→ 20 Guangdong Lu
Tel. 6350 9988
Daily 5pm–2am
Same owners as the restaurant above. The large bay window here also provides unbeatable views of the Bund. Inside, the style is Art Deco meets Hollywood, with elaborate cocktails and a daring cultural program: readings, chamber music, cabaret.

Bund 18 complex (**A** F3)
→ 1 Zhongshan Dongyilu
Tel. 6339 1199 Bar Rouge:
daily 6.30pm–2.30am (4am Fri-Sat); www.bund18.com
The very cool Bund 18 complex opened in 2004 and houses, on the sixth floor, Shanghai's classiest cocktail bar. With a vast terrace over the Bund (reserve if you want a table inside by a window) and striking scarlet decor, Bar Rouge is a great spot, though mostly patronized by foreigners, and can get

very loud as the evening goes on. It stands above Sens and Bund, the first restaurant in China to be run by three-star Michelin chefs, the French Pourcel twins (though, sadly, they are not often on site). Reserve here too (tel. 6323 9898).

The Room with a View
顶层画廊 (**A** D3)
→ *479 Nanjing Donglu*
Tel. 6352 0256
Daily 3–10pm
A small room on the 11th floor, favored by local arty types, not only for its stunning views but also for its laid-back ambience. It has an exhibition space for paintings, photos and architectural projects.

Heavenlies (**A** E4)
→ *88 Henan Zhonglu*
Tel. 6335 1888 Daily
7am–midnight (1am Fri-Sat)
A glass roof covers the bar of the Hotel Westin, with its extravagantly curved daybeds, flanked by water and set off by a luminous staircase. Wines from all over the world served by the glass, champagne and coffee with liquors.

Barbarossa (**A** A4)
→ *231 Nanjing Xilu*
Tel. 6318 0220
Daily 11am–2am
This four-storey, Middle Eastern-styled lounge bar

in the heart of the People's Square is quite a magnificent venue for a drink. Very popular for its themed evenings and DJ sets on the rooftop terrace giving onto the lake. Dining area on the first floor; great list of drinks in the bars; hookah pipes.

CABARET, THEATER

Yifu Theater
逸夫舞台 (**A** B4)
→ *701 Fuzhou Lu*
Tel. 6322 5294 Show 7.15pm,
several nights a week;
shop: daily 8.30am–8pm
All China's most famous companies perform here, the best venue in town for traditional theater: Beijing and Shanghai opera, *kunqu*, etc. Recordings of popular melodies are on sale at the entrance.

The Great World Entertainment Center
大世界 (**A** C4)
→ *1 Xizang Nanlu*
Tel. 6374 6703
Daily 9am–9.30pm
This entertainment complex helped define the legend of 1920s' Shanghai, with its cafés, restaurants, gambling, movies and theater. It is once again a fun palace with acrobatics, karaoke, movies, Chinese opera...

SHOPPING

Nanjing donglu
南京东路 (**A** B3-E2)
The city's most famous shopping street.

Shanghai No. 1 Department Store (**A** B3)
上海市第一百货商店
→ *830 Nanjing Donglu*
Tel. 6322 3344
Daily 9.30am–10pm
The ground floor suits bargain-hunters, but the prices on the upper stories are for a wealthier Chinese clientele.

Bao Da Xiang Shopping for Kids (**A** B3)
→ *685 Nanjing Donglu*
Tel. 6352 2624
Daily 9.30am–10pm
Everything for children: from clothes to furniture, toys and video games.

Sashi Lu Market
中央商场 (**A** E3)
→ *Sashi Yilu, Sashi Erlu*
Daily 8am–6pm
Two small streets crammed with stands selling all kinds of wares: fruit and vegetables, statuettes of Buddha, traditional clothes, etc.

Shanghai Antique & Curio Store (**A** E3)
上海市古玩市场
→ *238 Guangdong Lu*
Tel. 6321 4697
Daily 9am–5pm
Well-known antique store

selling lacquered screens, sculpted jade, porcelain, genuinely ancient furniture or good reproductions.

Shanghai's City of Books
上海书城 (**A** D3)
→ *465 Fuzhou Lu*
Tel. 6352 2222
Daily 9am–9pm
The biggest of all the Fuzhou Lu bookstores. On the top floor is a quiet bar, with CDs and some foreign magazines and books.

Opera props store
上海南泰戏剧服
装用品有限公司 (**A** D3)
→ *654–658 Guangdong Lu*
Daily 9am–5pm
All the props and costumes typical of Chinese opera: long peacock feathers, embroidered bags and spectacular robes.

Three on the Bund (**A** F3)
→ *Tel. 6321 7733*
www.threeonthebund.com
The outstanding seven-storey building at no. 3, the Bund, is a 21st-century urban symbol. Everything is at hand to keep you pleased and entertained – shopping (with Armani on the ground floor), pampering (at the only Evian spa outside France), dining (at Jean-Georges, a gourmet restaurant owned by the famous J-G Vongerichten) and culture (at the Shanghai Gallery of Art).

↑ Map F

↓ Map E

HUANGPU

HUANGPU

ZHONGSHAN DONGYILU

★ CUSTOM HOUSE
海关大楼

★ BANK OF SHANGHAI
上海银行

HANKOU LU

JIUJIANG LU

HENAN LU

NANJING DONGLU

★ PEACE HOTEL SOUTH
和平饭店南楼

SASHI LU

SUZHOU

JIANGXI BEILU

JIMIJIANG LU

NANJING DONG RD
CENTRAL
HENAN RD

BUND SIGHTSEEING TUNNEL

CHEN YI MONUMENT

BUND MONUMENT

★ PEACE HOTEL
和平饭店

DIANCHI LU

TIANJIN LU

BO LU

★ BANK OF CHINA
中国银行

2

NINGBO LU

JIANGXI ZHONGLU

BANK OF CHINA

★ COMMERCIAL INDUSTRIAL &
中国工商银行

FRIENDSHIP STORE

HUANGPU PARK

BEIJING DONGLU

HENAN ZHONGLU

YUANMINGYUAN LU

TOURIST INFORMATION

SHANGHAI PEOPLE'S HEROES MEMORIAL

WAIBAIDU BRIDGE

HUQIU LU

SICHUAN ZHONGLU

JIANGXI ZHONGLU

XIANG GANG LU

NANSUZHOULU

CHANGZHI LU

HUANGPULU

WUSONG LU

NANSUZHOULU

SUZHOU

BEISUZHOULU

BEISUZHOULU

1

DAMING LU

MINGHANG LU

WUCHANG LU

GHANG LU

EMELU

ZHAPU LU

TIANTONG LU

PEOPLE'S HOSPITAL No 1

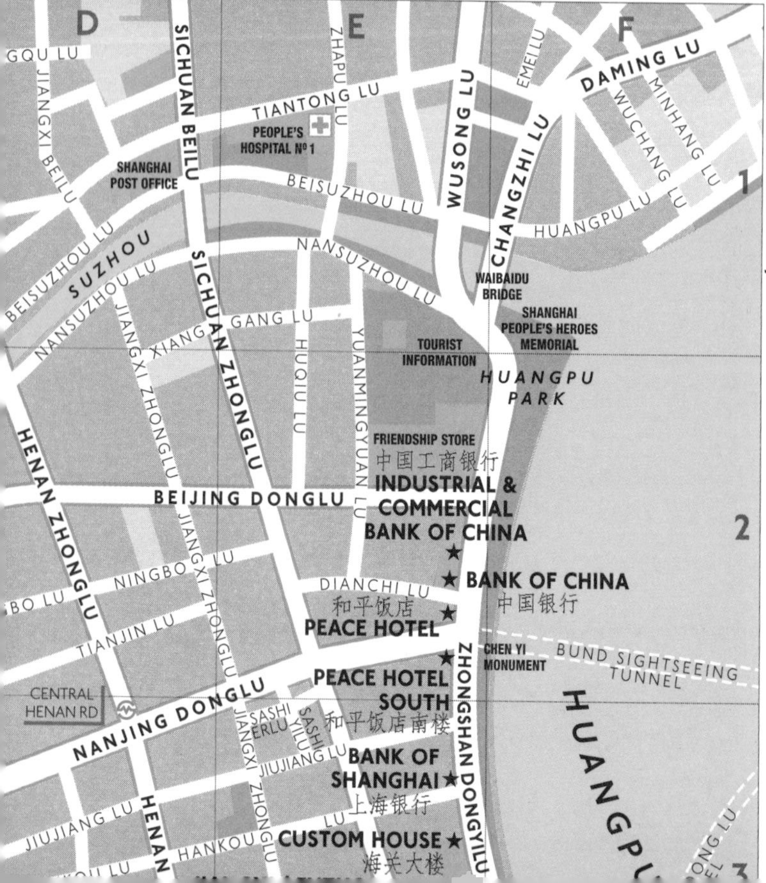

SICHUAN BEILU

SHANGHAI POST OFFICE

SICHUAN BEILU

JIANGXI BEILU

GOU LU

F

E

D

BANK OF SHANGHAI

HOTEL SOUTH

Map C →

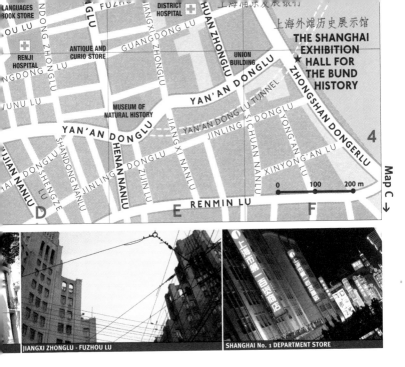

LANGUAGES BOOK STORE

RENJI HOSPITAL

ANTIQUE AND CURIO STORE

DISTRICT HOSPITAL

UNION BUILDING

THE SHANGHAI EXHIBITION ★ HALL FOR THE BUND HISTORY

上海外滩历史展示馆

MUSEUM OF NATURAL HISTORY

YAN'AN DONGLU

YAN'AN DONGLU

YAN'AN DONG LU TUNNEL

YAN'AN DONG LU

4

RENMIN LU

0   100   200 m

JIANGXI ZHONGLU - FUZHOU LU

SHANGHAI No. 1 DEPARTMENT STORE

---

stoms House (A E3)
Zhongshan Dongyilu
ustoms House (Palmer
er, 1927) still keeps
watch on the comings
oings on the Huangpu
The bells in the clock
, which supposedly
the hours with the
notes as Big Ben,
from the Palace of
minster and were
ed to mark Queen
eth II's visit
anghai in 1986.
**anghai Pudong
opment Bank (A** E3)
Zhongshan Dongyilu
ongest building on the
was from 1923 to
the headquarters of

the Hong Kong & Shanghai
Bank (then the second
biggest bank in the world)
before being converted into
the city hall. Although a red
flag still flies from its dome,
this neoclassical building
(Palmer & Turner), reverted
to its former use in 1995.
Admire the octagonal
lobby (with allegorical
representations of eight of
the world's cities) and the
huge, ornately decorated
banking room.
★ **Shanghai Exhibition
Hall for the Bund History
(A** F4)
→ *1 Zhongshan Dongyilu*
Tel. 6321 6542
Daily 9am–noon, 1–5pm

The former lighthouse of
the French Concession
(1907), tucked between
the shore and a raised
promenade jutting over
the estuary, is now a small
museum chronicling the
history of the Bund with
photos from the first half
of the 20th century.
★ **Jiangxi zhonglu –
Fuzhou lu (A** E3)
This crossroads, close to
the bustling port, is the site
of the former Shanghai
Municipal Council (1919),
the governing body of the
International Settlement.
The junction is lined by a
fine set of four buildings
(two of them identical).

★ **Shanghai N°1
Department Store (A** B3)
→ *830 Nanjing Donglu*
Tel. 6322 3344
Daily 9.30am–10pm
The newest of the
department stores on this
busy shopping street (Jitai
Kwan, Chu & Yang, 1936)
also marks the start of its
pedestrian section. It was
the first Chinese store to
install escalators and even
today is a symbol of the
consumer society. However,
its nighttime illumination is
restrained, compared to its
neighbors bedecked with
neon signs. The corner of
the block is clad with
elegant enamel tiles.

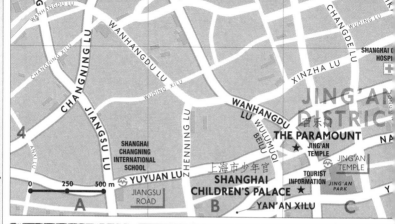

THE PARAMOUNT
JING'AN DISTRICT
SHANGHAI CHANGNING INTERNATIONAL SCHOOL
JIANGSU ROAD
SHANGHAI CHILDREN'S PALACE ★
JING'AN TEMPLE
JING'AN TEMPLE
TOURIST INFORMATION
JING'AN PARK
YAN'AN XILU
SHANGHAI (HOSPI
上海市少年官
0 250 500 m

THE PARAMOUNT

SHANGHAI CHILDREN'S PALACE

★ Shanghai Urban Planning Exhibition Center (B F4)

→ 100 Renmin Dadao
Tel. 6318 4477
Daily 9am–5pm

This futuristic building was opened in 2000 to present the history of the city and its ambitious planning projects. The slogan of the day is displayed on a banner spanning the huge foyer, while the third floor houses the museum's highlight: a fascinating giant scale model (6,450 square feet), showing what the city will look like in 2020 – with more than one thousand skyscrapers. There are great views of the People's Square from the top floor.

★ Shanghai Grand Theater (B F4)

→ 300 Renmin Dadao
Tel. 6386 8686
www.shgtheatre.com

Following the principles of feng shui (geomancy), this theater (ARTE Charpentier, 1998) has no opening to the west – a direction associated with death. It has, however, a stupendous arc-shaped roof, glass walls, an impressive foyer of 21,500 square feet paved with rare marble, and three auditoria: the Studio Theater (300 seats),

Drama Theater (750 seats) and Lyric Theater (1,800 seats), all with state-of-the-art equipment. Opera, concerts and ballet performances.

★ Park Hotel (B F3)

→ 170 Nanjing Xilu
Tel. 6327 5225

The celebrated Park Hotel – built by Laszlo Hudec in 1933 next to the racecourse, which belongs to the concessions – is now the site of the People's Square (Renmin Guangchang). For many years it was the city's highest building (280 feet, 23 floors); although it has long since been surpassed, its pyramidal roof and dark polished bricks h lost none of their Art-D type elegance.

★ Shanghai Museum (B F4)

→ 201 Renmin Dadao
Tel. 6372 3500
Daily 9am–5pm;
www.shanghaimuseum.
en/index.asp

To the south of the Pe Square, opposite the c hall, the layout of the Shanghai Museum (19 reflects the principles c Chinese cosmogony: t square base in the ima of the Earth and the ro rounded like the sky de the two poles of huma

JIAOZHOU

ANYUAN LU

CHANGSHOU LU

CARREFOUR WUNING STORE

TAENTS MARKET WUNING PAPER

PUXIONG LU

SHANXI BEILU

XIKANG LU

ANY

CHANGDE LU

WUNING

JADE BUDDHA TEMPLE
玉佛禅寺

CHANGHUA

CHANGSHOU LU

CHANGSHOU PARK

XIKANG LU

JIANGNING LU

XIKANG LU

SUZHOU

ZHONGSHAN BEILU

DONGXIN LU

ZHENPING ROAD

PUTUO DISTRICT

ZHONGTAN ROAD

ZHONGSHAN BEI

JIAOTONG LU

HUAXIN

SHIQUAN LU

LANGAO LU

GUANGXIN LU

HUACHI LU

GUANNONG

FUCUN LU

TONGCHUAN LU

C

B

A

1

2

SHANGHAI GRAND THEATRE

SHANGHAI URBAN PLANNING EXHIBITION CENTER

PARK HOTEL

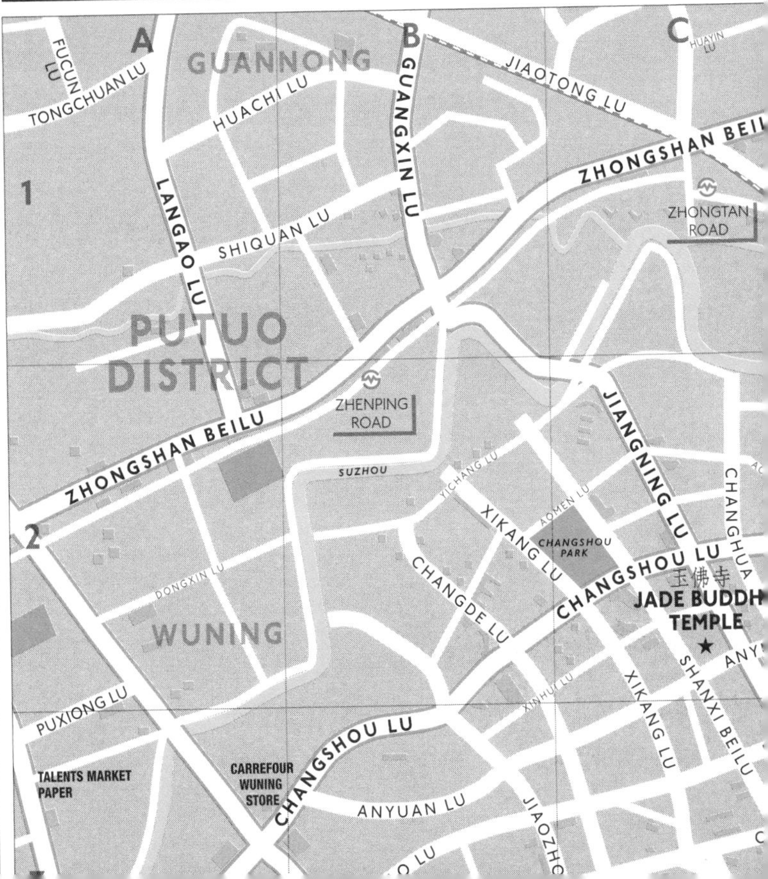

Renmin Guangchang (the People's Square) and its temples of Culture, appropriately organized around the City Hall, form the heart of modern-day Shanghai. To the west runs Nanjing Xilu, its ultramodern shopping malls occasionally giving way to a colorful little square or a few colonial villas. In the Zhabei district, on the opposite bank of the Suzhou, an enchanting tea market nestles behind the Shanghai Railway Station, where people from all over China disembark in search of a better life in the big city.

YUFO TANG
WUJIANG LU

RESTAURANTS

Yufo Tang (vegetarian restaurant of the Jade Buddha Temple)
玉佛塘 (**B** C2)
→ 170 Anyuan Lu
Daily 8am–5pm
A corpulent Buddha in the middle of the dining room bestows blessings on his devotees as they eat off the large communal tables. Healthy food in a simple, convivial atmosphere. Fantastic noodles and mushrooms soup. ¥5.

Wujiang Lu
吴江路 (**B** DE4)
→ Daily 10am–11pm
This street has long been considered one of the best places to eat in Shanghai. Throughout the day passersby stop at its stands or enter its eating houses for snacks of Wuhanese duck, typical local ravioli, Beijing fruit coated with caramel, etc. Dish ¥15.

Bi Feng Tang
避风塘 (**B** C4)
→ 1333 Nanjing Xilu
Tel. 6279 0738
Daily 10am–5pm
Fishermen's clothes hanging on the walls, nets stretched across the ceiling and tables set under straw canopies:

fish and seafood are the order of the day here, as well as Cantonese dishes, all served by waiters in traditional costumes. Carte ¥40.

Café Montmartre (**B** C3)
→ 537 Haifang Lu
Tel. 5404 7658
Daily 10am–midnight
One of the first French restaurants to have opened in Shanghai. The atmosphere inside is distinctly European, with jazz music, decor evoking a French bistro, a menu offering Mediterranean dishes and crêpes to ensure authenticity. Carte 75 ¥.

1221 一二二一 (**B** B4)
→ 1221 Yan'an Xilu
Tel. 6213 6585
Daily 11am–2pm, 5–11pm
Only a tiny sign at the back of the courtyard of no. 1221 indicates that a gourmet restaurant lies within. An intimate setting for elaborate Chinese dishes, washed down with excellent Dragon Seal wine. Carte ¥100.

Meilongzhen (**B** C4)
→ 1081 Nanjing Xilu
Tel. 6256 6688
Daily 11am–2pm, 5–10pm
One of the oldest and most celebrated restaurants in town, Meilongzhen opened

PLAZA 66

SHANGART

its doors in 1938. Sichuan and Shanghai specialties are served in a traditional marble and wood decor. Carte ¥100.

Kathleen's Fifth (B F4)
→ *325 Nanjing Xilu*
Tel. 6327 2221
Daily 11am–2am
Kathleen Lau, the founder of the famous monthly, *That's Shanghai*, has opened her fifth restaurant on the roof of the Shanghai Art Museum. Chinese and European cooking, and a fusion of the two. The outlandish design and lighting is the work of Liu Dong. Huge terrace with a panoramic view of People's Square. Carte ¥200.

BARS, CLUBS

Malone's (B C4)
→ *255 Tongren Lu*
Tel. 6247 2400
Daily 10am–3am
Wishing you were home watching that important baseball or soccer game? Come to Malone's, as chances are it will be shown on the big screen. Imported beers, generous Mexican, Italian and American dishes (the burgers are particularly good). Relaxed during the day, noisier in the

evening. Live concerts at the weekend. Carte ¥150.

Always Cafe (B C4)
→ *1528 Nanjing Xilu*
Tel. 6247 8333
Daily 11am–2am
Less than 200 yards from the Jing An Temple, in the most famous street in the city, the peaceful Always Café has a decor meant to recall Shanghai in the 1930s.

Jazz 37 (B D4)
→ *500 Weihai Lu*
Tel. 3218 6955
Mon-Sat 9pm–1am
An elegant yet cozy club on the 37th (top) floor of the Four Seasons Hotel, with live jazz music. Long, brightly lit bar, stunning inlaid parquet floor and breathtaking, almost 360° panoramic views. A wide selection of wines and good cocktails is available.

Mint (B C4)
→ *333 Tongren Lu*
Tel. 6247 9666
Sun-Thu 11am–2am
(4am Fri-Sat)
Popular bar and nightclub with a striking long table, walls lined with purple velvet drapes and deep, comfortable sofas. From 10pm, renowned DJs set the tone with lounge music (Sun-Wed) or techno-house (Thu-Sat).

THEATER

Majestic Theater
美琪大戏院 **(B** D4)
→ *66 Jiangning Lu*
Tel. 6217 4409
An eclectic program (Chinese operas, musical comedies, ballets) in one of the city's biggest theaters (1,328 seats), built in 1941.

ART GALLERIES, SHOPPING

Shanghai Museum Art Company (B F4)
→ *201 Renmin Dadao*
Tel. 6372 3523
Daily 9.30am–5pm
Here you can buy a reproduction of a work of art on display in the museum. The store also stocks a large selection of art books in several languages, calligraphy material (brushes and ink stones), painted or hand-written scrolls, etc.

Plaza 66 (B D4)
→ *1266 Nanjing Xilu*
Daily 10am–10pm
The second highest building in the city, and one of the least frenetic of Shanghai's shopping malls, with swanky customers strolling from one store selling international labels to

the next: Louis Vuitton, Karl Lagerfeld, Gianni Versace, Christian Dior, etc.

Store of the Jade Buddha Temple (B C2)
→ *170 Anyuan Lu*
Daily 8am–5pm
In the pavilion of the reclining Buddha, you can buy his portrait in a number of mediums, such as medallions, pendants, statuettes, paintings and prints.

Moganshan Lu 莫干山路
Old factory buildings now occupied by art galleries showcasing the best in contemporary Chinese design.

Eastlink
东廊艺术 **(B** D2)
→ *50 Moganshan Lu, bldg 6*
Tel. 6276 9932
Tue-Sun 10am–6pm
In 2001 Eastlink, a gallery founded in 1999 by Li Liang, took over the entire fifth floor of this factory. It shows installations, painting, photography, etc.

Shanghart
香格纳画廊 **(B** D2)
→ *50 Moganshan Lu, bldg 16*
Tel. 6359 3923 (by appt)
All the reserves of the famous gallery on Gaolan Lu **(D** E2) are stored in this old warehouse.

Also on Mogashan Road Design Center, YB1 Galery, Number D store and more.

ZHEJIANG BEILU

QUFU LU

HAINING LU

TIANMU DONGLU

XINZHA

ZHA LU

CHENGDU BEILU

NANSUZHOU LU

NANSUZHOU LU

KAIFENG LU

GUOQING LU

XINYIMIAN LU

WUZHEN LU

DATONG LU

PINGXING LU

SUZHOU

SH

SHANG'AN

HANZHONG ROAD

HENGFENG LU

HANZHONG LU

DATONG LU

HENGFENG LU

HEBIN CENTER

YANGCUO LU

GONGHE LU

TIANMU XILU

KERRY EVERBRIGHT CITY

JIATONG PARK

2

JIXOTONG LU

QIUJIANG LU

YONGXING LANG LU

YONGXING LU

ZHONGXING LU

GONGHE XINLU

SHANGHAI RAILWAY STATION

SHANGHAI RAILWAY STATION

HENGFENG BEILU

ZHONGXING LU

ZHONGXING LU

ZHONGHUA XINLU

DATONG LU

ZHONGXING LU

HUMEN LU

XIZANG BEILU

ZHABEI DISTRICT

ZHABEI DISTRICT CENTRAL HOSPITAL

ZHONGHUA XINLU

HUTAI LU

CHINESE MEDICINE HOSPITAL

ZHONGXING DONGLU

ZHIJIANG ZHONGLU

1

ZHIJIANG XILU

PUSHAN LU

ZHIYUAN LU

XIZANG BEILU

ZHONGSHAN BEILU

QINGYUN LU

E

XIAOTIAN LU

PUSHAN LU

D

HAI ART MUSEUM

SHANGHAI MUSEUM

Map text:

XINZHA LU — BEIJING XILU — 国际饭店 — PARK HOTEL ★ — SHANGHAI No.1 DEPARTMENT STORE

SHIMEN N°1 ROAD — WESTGATE MALL — WUJIANG LU — 上海美术馆 — SHANGHAI ART MUSEUM ★ — PEOPLE'S SQUARE — RENMIN GUANGCHANG (PEOPLE'S SQUARE) — 上海城市规划展示馆 — SHANGHAI URBAN PLANNING EXHIBITION CENTER

SHANTA BEILU — MAOMING BEILU — SHIMEN YILU — SHANGHAI TV STATION — JIANGYIN LU — 上海大剧院 — SHANGHAI GRAND THEATER ★ — RENMIN DADAO — 上海博物馆 — SHANGHAI MUSEUM ★

WEIHAI LU — HUANGPI BEILU — WUSHENG LU — SHANGHAI CONCERT HALL

JULU LU — YAN'AN DONGLU — XIZANG ZHONGLU

Map D →

4

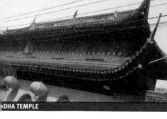

DHA TEMPLE

JADE BUDDHA TEMPLE

...ce. The ten thematic ...es, spread over four ... contain priceless ... treasures from ...e and Classical ...paintings, ...res, ceramics, ...e, jade, coins and ...nore). Don't miss ...ection of bronze ...res, including pieces ...back to the Shang ...y (18th–11th ...es BC), or the ...ely rare examples of ...ckery (12th century) ...orcelain gallery).

...nghai Art
...m (B F4)
...Nanjing Xilu
...2 2829

Daily 9am–4pm
The old horseracing clubhouse, built in a neoclassical style in 1935, now serves to exhibit contemporary Chinese art. All today's top artists have had at least one show in the two beautiful galleries on the ground floor.

★ The Paramount (B C4)
→ *218 Yuyuan Lu*
Tel. 6249 8866
Daily 1pm–1am
At the crossroads of three major boulevards, the city's most famous pre-war dance hall (Yang Ximiao, 1932) has reverted to its role as a nightclub after a

period serving as a theater. Two large dance floors with bandstands are overlooked by colorful mezzanines.

★ Shanghai Children's Palace (B C4)
→ *64 Yan'an Xilu*
Tel. 6248 1850
Well-preserved statues surround the villa built in 1924 by Ellis Kadoorie, a member of a prominent local Jewish family. Since 1953 the old Marble Hall, topped with a red star, has been a center where children can study music, ballet, gymnastics or other disciplines. Many of them are hand-picked prodigies,

and they perform regularly in the opulent ballroom.

★ Jade Buddha Temple (B C2)
→ *170 Anyuan Lu*
Daily 8am–5pm
Although the crowds that flock to the Jade Buddha Temple (Yufo Si) include a few worshippers, they mainly comprise tourists eager to see the two Buddhas in (false) jade brought over from Burma in 1882: the bronze Bodhisattvas, dating back to the northern Wei (4th–6th centuries), and its graceful Guanyin (goddess of fertility) carved out of jujube wood.

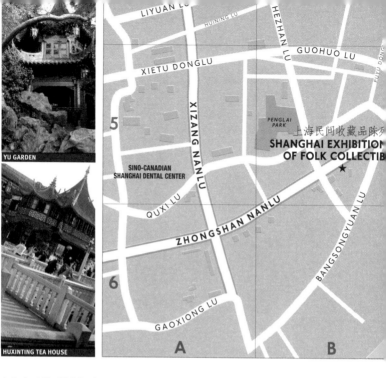

YU GARDEN

HUXINTING TEA HOUSE

On the map: LIYUAN LU, HUINING LU, HEZHAN LU, GUOHUO LU, PUDONG, XIETU DONGLU, XIZANG NANLU, PENGLAI PARK, 上海民间收藏品陈列, SHANGHAI EXHIBITION OF FOLK COLLECTIB, SINO-CANADIAN SHANGHAI DENTAL CENTER, QUXI LU, ZHONGSHAN NANLU, BANGSONGYUAN LU, GAOXIONG LU

5

6

A   B

★ **Ancient City Wall** (C A2)
→ 269 Dajing Lu
Tel. 6385 2443
Daily 9am–4pm
A maze of corridors, a temple dedicated to Guan Yu (a general from the Han dynasty immortalized as the god of War) and some galleries presenting the history of the Old Town. This is all that remains of the round wall, lined with a canal that was built in the 16th century to protect the city from Japanese pirates. The rest of the wall was demolished in 1912 because its countless rat-infested sluiceways were a danger to public health.

★ **Yu Garden** (C B1-2)
→ 173 Yuyuan Lu
Daily 8.30am–5pm
Pan Yundan, the governor of Sichuan, created this Garden of Joy (Yu Yuan) for his father in the 16th century. The land was later sold to guilds of merchants. All the elements expected from the garden of a prominent social figure are found here: streams, lotus ponds, bonsais, bizarrely shaped rocks conjuring up images of mountains, a pool evoking seas and lakes – all designed to create reproductions of famous natural settings on a reduced scale.

★ **Huxinting Tea House** (C B2)
→ 257 Yuyuan Lu
Tel. 6355 8270 Daily 6.30am (10am Fri-Sun)–midnight
Chinese tea houses were once luxurious meeting places with musicians, storytellers and courtesans. The oldest one in Shanghai (1855) occupies a pavilion in the Yu Garden, and is reputed to be the inspiration for the tea house depicted on 'willow pattern' plates. The pavilion 'in the middle of the lake' is linked to the shore by a bridge with nine zigzags intended to disorient evil spirits, who can only travel in a

straight line.

★ **City God Temple** (
→ 249 Fangbang Zhon
Tel. 6386 8649
Daily 8.30am–4pm
Before entering the Cit God Temple (Chenghu Miao), visitors salute t four cardinal points, b going on to invoke the of Health and meditate front of an effigy of Qir Yubo, a civil servant fro the Yuan dynasty who been converted into Shanghai's protective

★ **Shanghai Xiaotao Mosque** (C B3)
→ 52 Xiaotaoyuan Jie
Tel. 6377 5442
Daily 5am–8pm

C

YU GARDEN

CITY GOD TEMPLE

ANCIENT CITY WALL

LUJIABANG LU

SHANGHAI OBS. & GVN. HOSPITAL

ZHONGHUA LU

FANGXIE LU

PENGLAI LU

NINGHE LU

HENAN NANLU

XINYONG'AN LU

WENMIAO LU

XIUNHOU LU

SHANGHAI CONFUCIAN TEMPLE

XUEGONG JIE

SHANGHAI XIAOTAOYUAN MOSQUE
上海小桃园清真寺

FUXING DONGLU

ZHONGHUA LU

XIAOTAOYUAN JIE

FUXING DONGLU

XIZANG NANLU

DONGTAI LU

LIUHEKOU LU

HUANGPU DISTRICT

FANGBANG ZHONGLU

SANPAILOU LU

HENAN NANLU

LUXIANGYUAN LU

DAJING LU

RENMIN LU

FANGBANG ZHONGLU

★ YU GARDEN
豫园

NANFENG CULTURAL OR HISTORICAL RELICS TRADE MARKET

BAIYUNGUAN TEMPLE

上海白云观大殿图

★ ANCIENT CITY WALL
上海古城墙大境阁

DAJING LU

FUYOU LU

RENMIN LU

ZHEJIANG NANLU

JINLING DONGLU

MUSEUM OF NATURAL HISTORY

Old Town (Nanshi)

In the 18th century the fortified city, the oldest inhabited part of Shanghai, started to take fuller advantage of the resources of the Huangpu and its proximity to the sea to turn itself into a thriving port. Shanghai's reputation as a trading center remains, to this day, unchallenged. The Old Town (Nanshi) retains on its narrow and crowded streets, markets selling food, textiles, birds and plants. Fortunately, the frenzied construction boom that has transformed the heart of the historic city has left the area surrounding the Confucian Temple relatively unscathed.

DONGJIADU LU

HUXINTING TEA HOUSE

RESTAURANTS

Dongjiadu Lu
董家渡路 (**C** D4)
→ 150–160 Dongjiadu Lu
Daily 5am–7pm
These good-value stalls are extremely popular with both customers and traders from the silk market. They specialize in noodles, either in soup or with pork. There are a few tables inside for people with more time on their hands. Dish ¥5.

Shanghai Classical Restaurant (**C** B1)
→ 242 Fuyou Lu
Tel. 6311 1777
Daily 11am–2pm, 5–10pm
Close to the Yu Garden, an enormous dining room on the building's first floor offers classic dishes from the local repertoire: pig's stomach, tofu with crabs, shrimps with pine nuts, etc. Carte ¥20.

BARS

Huxinting Tea House
湖心亭茶馆 (**C** B2)
→ 257 Yuyuan Lu
Tel. 6355 8270
Mon-Thu 6.30am–midnight;
Fri-Sun 10am–midnight
Climb the steep staircase to the first floor and revel in the beautiful view of the Yu Garden. Classical Chinese music in the background, and quail's eggs as a complement to your cup of tea. See also next page

Song Yun Lu Wine Shop (**C** B2)
→ 98 Yuyuan Lu
Tel. 136 6162 9572
Daily 8.30am–9pm
This tiny, gaudily decorated bar sells divine fresh fruit juices. Quench your thirst with either orange, apple, kiwi, strawberry, carrot, celery or apple.

Shanghai Guoji
上海国际 (**C** B3)
→ 42-46 Xuegong Jie
Tel. 6376 1072
Daily, 24 hrs
Animated poker games on the ground floor, while upstairs a fabulous terrace overlooks the peaceful garden of the Confucian Temple, with its pond full of fish. Small selection of teas, and the owner will rustle up a meal if you are hungry.

SHOPPING

Dongtai Lu flea market
董家渡路织品市 (**C** A3)
→ Dongtai Lu, Liuhekou Lu
Daily 10.30am–5.30pm
You can find everything here, from souvenir statuettes to copies of Qing vases, seals with

JIA JIE MARKET   **WAICANGQIAO JIE TEXTILE MARKET**   **SHANGHAI TAN SHANG SHA**

stylized characters, fascinating portraits of Mao and propaganda posters, silk lanterns, ceramic chopsticks, colorful earthenware and many other fabulous would-be presents.

Bird and plant market
上海花鸟鱼虫交易市场 (**C** A3)

→ 4405 Xizang Nanlu
Daily 8am–6pm

Plants and flowers are on display on the sidewalk in front of the covered market; inside are the caged birds (swallows, canaries, pigeons, parrots, etc.), fish, rabbits and chickens wandering around freely; plus tapes of recorded birdsongs.

Dajing Lu market
大境路市场 (**C** A2)

→ 150-160 Dajing Lu, Luxiangyuan Lu
Daily 5am–6pm

One of the city's biggest food markets, where you can buy fish and other aquatic creatures (crabs, sea snakes, frogs), but also chicken, Beijing duck, spices, bread, ravioli, tea and tofu.

Zhuangjia jie market
庄家街市场 (**C** B3)

→ Daily 10am–8pm

A small market in an alleyway near the Confucian Temple, with

baskets full of fruit and vegetables set out on the ground.

Waicangqiao jie textile market
外仓桥街织品市场 (**C** C3-4)

→ Waicangqiao Jie, Wangjiamatou Lu
Daily 8am–5pm

Not far from the market above, everything required for making clothes: fabric sold by the meter, buttons, threads and zippers. Also domestic linen, trousers, swimming costumes, etc.

Second-hand book market
古书市场 (**C** A3)

→ 215 Wenmiao Lu
Sun 8am–4pm

Every Sunday two courtyards in the venerable Confucian Temple are taken over by the colorful parasols of this market. On sale are fashion magazines, romantic photo novels, manga magazines, encyclopedias, specialized international magazines, and more.

Lujiabang Lu textile market (**C** C4)

→ 399 Lujiabang Lu (corner of Nancan Jie)
Daily 8am–6.30pm

Wonderful, large covered market over four floors, with a vast array of colors and fabrics from which

you can order pretty much anything at highly attractive prices (two-piece suit for ¥500). Nearly every stall has a highly skilled tailor waiting for you to show him one of your favorites piece of clothing, or a cut-out from a magazine, to create its exact copy for you to pick up two days later.

Liyunge Shanzhuang
丽云阁扇庄 (**C** B2)

→ 35 Yuyuan Laolu
Tel. 6355 9999 Daily 9am–9pm (10pm Fri-Sat)

This shop originally opened in 1880, and sells fans in a seemingly endless range of materials and designs, such as paper, wood, cloth or feathers. The fan might be designed in a single piece, and will either be carved, embroidered or painted.

Shanghai Tonghanchun Traditional Medicine Store
上海童涵春堂 (**C** B2)

→ 20 Yuyuan Xinlu
Tel. 6355 0308 Daily 8.30am–9pm (10pm Fri-Sat)

The largest traditional pharmacy in Shanghai, selling ginseng roots, medicinal herbs, dried fruit and moxas. A small room is devoted to European pharmaceutical products.

Yixuan Chazhuang
艺轩茶庄 (**C** B2)

→ Corner of Sanpailou Lu and Zhujin Lu. Daily 8am–6pm

It is impossible to resist the effusive invitation of Mrs Sun. Take some time and sit down to drink one of the many varieties of tea displayed in her stall.

Wen Xue Bi Chao Pu
文学币钞铺 (**C** A3)

→ 173 Wenmiao Lu
Tel. 136 1180 6053
Daily 10am–5pm

Tucked away in a corner of the enclosure of the Confucian Temple, this tiny shop is a meeting place for coin collectors.

Antique dealers on Fangbang zhonglu (**C** B2)

→ Near the corner of Henan Nanlu. Daily 8am–8pm

The antique dealers congregate around the large gate guarded by two dragons. You'll find here traditional musical instruments, Yixing teapots, carpets, pottery and furniture. Beware, some items are more antique than others!

Shanghai Tan Shang Sha
上海滩上纱 (**C** B1)

→ 388 Renmin Lu
Tel. 6333 1688
Daily 7am–5pm

A gallery with small stalls selling clothing accessories (ribbons, buttons, etc.).

↑ Map F

BAIYUNGUAN TEMPLE

SHANGHAI CONFUCIAN TEMPLE

XIAOTAOYUAN MOSQUE
SHANGHAI

1343

4

3

2

1

D

C

↓ Map A

JINMAO TOWER

HUANGPU

YINCHENG ZHONGLU
YINCHENG NANLU
FUCHENG LU
YINCHENG XILU
BINJIANG DADAO
FUCHENG LU
DONGCHANG LU
PUMIN LU

DONGJIADU LU
WANGJIAMATOU LU
WALCANGQIAO JIE
MIEZHU LU
ZIXIA LU

Waihong

WAIMA LU
BAIDU LU

FUXING DONGLU
FUXING DONGLU TUNNEL

LAODAPING LONG
DONGJIE

ZHONGHUA LU

XUNDAO JIE

N JIE

DONGLU

TEA HOUSE

TEMPLE

SHAN DONGERLU

ZHONGS

LU

HUANGPU

WAMA LU

南浦大桥
NANPU BRIDGE
★

SHANGHAI HAISU ART
DESIGN & INSTITUTE

5

LONGYANG
LU

6

0   200   400 m

C   D

**SHANGHAI EXHIBITION HALL
OF FOLK COLLECTIBLES**

NANPU BRIDGE

losque of the Garden
Small Peaches
) can be spotted from
g Donglu, thanks to
inaret topped with
scent moon and the
s painted in green,
e entrance is tucked
at the end of a back
Inside is a huge
r room facing to
toward Mecca.

**anghai Confucian
le (C** A3)
5 Wenmiao Lu
77 9826
8.30am–3.30pm
series of courtyards
alls, isolated from its
ing surroundings by
walls, deserves a

prolonged visit. The main
pavilion contains a statue
of Master Kong (c.551–
479 BC), the subject of an
official cult until 1927, which
still serves as a model and
protector for scholars. It is
common for students to
inscribe their name and the
university they want to enter
on a piece of red cloth and
then attach it to the large
tree in front of the statue.
The pagoda in the garden
dates from the 18th century.

**★ Baiyunguan
Temple (C** A3)
→ 100 Xilinhou Lu
Tel. 6328 7236
Daily 8.30am–4pm
This Taoist sanctuary with

red-ocher walls shelters
under the branches of a
huge old tree. The Temple
of the White Clouds
(19th century) owes its
name to the 8,000 scrolls it
received from the temple of
that name in Beijing.
Terracotta soldiers on the
roofs keep watch, to ensure
that nothing disrupts the
serene atmosphere.

**★ Shanghai Exhibition
Hall of Folk Collectibles
(C** B5)
→ 1551 Zhongsan Nanlu
Tel. 6314 6453
Daily 9am–4pm
Once the headquarters of
a merchants' guild from
Fujian (1901), the Sanshan

Huigan has preserved its
wonderful theater (the
guild's annual party holds
dramatic performances). In
the halls, objects from the
city's key private collections:
cigarette lighters, models of
boats, propaganda posters,
crockery, etc.

★ Nanpu Bridge (C-D5)
→ Pedestrian access daily
8.30am–4pm
The first bridge over the
Huangpu (1991) connects
Puxi ('west of the river') with
Pudong ('east of the river').
The heavy flow of traffic
has to ascend a spiraled
access road to reach the
cable-stayed structure with
a span of 1,390 feet.

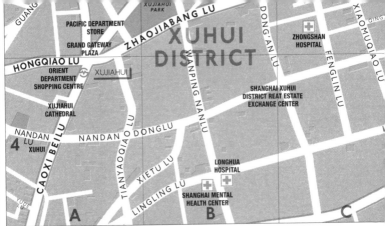

PACIFIC DEPARTMENT STORE
GRAND GATEWAY PLAZA
GUANG
XUJIAHUI PARK
ZHAOJIABANG LU
XUHUI DISTRICT
DONG'AN LU
XIAOMUQIAO LU
QING
ZHONGSHAN HOSPITAL
HONGQIAO LU
ORIENT DEPARTMENT SHOPPING CENTRE
XUJIAHUI
WANPING NANLU
SHANGHAI XUHUI DISTRICT REAT ESTATE EXCHANGE CENTER
FENGLIN LU
XUJIAHUI CATHEDRAL
NANDAN LU XUHUI
NANDAN O DONGLU
TIANYAOQIAO LU
XIETU LU
LINGLING LU
LONGHUA HOSPITAL
SHANGHAI MENTAL HEALTH CENTER
CAOXI BEILU
4
YUFE
A
B
C

RUIJIN GUEST HOUSE

SHANGHAI MUSEUM OF PUBLIC SECURITY

★ **Shanghai Museum of Sun Yat-sen's Former Residence** (**D** E2)
→ *7 Xiangshan Lu*
Tel. 6437 2954
Daily 9am–4.30pm
The first President of the Chinese Republic, Sun Yat-sen (1866–1925), and his wife, Soong Ching Ling, lived in this villa from 1920 to 1924, and his statue now holds court by the porch. Guided tours offer a glimpse of the private world of the founder of modern China, complete with some of his own furniture and private possessions.

★ **Fuxing Park** (**D** E2)
→ *22 Gaolan Lu*
Daily 6am–6pm

The plane tree originated in Yunan, but in the 18th century it was acclimatized in France, where it was systematically planted in towns and along the sides of roads. In 1909, when the French created the Fuxing Park, the circle was completed, because they made plane trees the star attraction. The park, whose entrance is unassuming, has become a popular place for locals to read by the pond or play mahjong or cards under the fragrant trees.

★ **Jinjiang Hotel and Grosvenor House** (**D** D1)
→ *59 Maoming Nanlu*
Tel. 6258 2582
Both integrated into the

Jinjiang Hotel complex, the Cathay Mansion Hotel (1929) and the residential block Grosvenor House (1935) formed part of a development project, financed by Victor Sassoon. The latter has conserved all its Art Deco panache: a huge porch with pillars embellished with bas-reliefs, and an impressive reception area with stylish wood paneling.

★ **Memorial for the First National Congress of the Communist Party of China** (**D** E1)
→ *374 Huangpi Nanlu*
Daily 9am–4pm
In a climate of increasing revolt against foreign

domination of China, 23, 1921 this *lilong* in French Concession wi the founding Congres the Communist Party attended by 13 Chine including Mao Zedon two representatives o Komintern. Photos, c and newspapers from period are on display

★ **Okura Garden H Shanghai** (**D** D1)
→ *58 Maoming Nanlu*
Tel. 6415 1111
This hotel was erecte 1986 on the site of t French Club (1925), a has incorporated so parts of the old build main staircase, with depicting languid wo

↓ Map B

SONG QINGLING'S RESIDENCE IN SHANGHAI
上海宋庆龄故居

SHANGHAI LIBRARY
上海图书馆

SILK COMMERCIAL

REGAL INTERNATIONAL EAST ASIA

INTERNATIONAL CHURCH

HENGSHAN ROAD

CREWSTEAK & SEAFOOD
BULL FIGHT

CHANGSHU ROAD

SHANGHAI HANGUANG CERAMIC GALLERY

HUASHAN HOSPITAL

EAST CHINA HOSPITAL

SHANGHAI CHILDREN'S PALACE

JING'AN PARK

JING'AN TEMPLE

THE PARAMOUNT

SHANGHAI EXHIBITION

SHANGHAI CHANGNING INTERNATIONAL SCHOOL

JIANGSU ROAD

Street labels: JIANGUO XILU, YUEYANG LU, TAIYUAN LU, ANTING LU, JIANGUO XILU, TIANGPING LU, HUASHAN LU, HUAIHAI XILU, SHANGHAI, RUIJING LU, WANPING LU, YUKING LU, GAO'AN LU, WULUMUQI NANLU, HENGSHAN, DONGPING LU, WUKANG LU, XINGUO LU, FENYANG LU, HUNAN LU, XINGXING LU, PINGWU LU, HUAIHAI ZHONGLU, YANQING LU, FUXING XILU, YOUYUAN LU, DONGHU LU, WULUMUQI ZHONGLU, CHANGSHU LU, HUASHAN LU, YAN'AN XILU, JULU LU, FUMIN LU, WULUMUQI BEILU, NANJING XILU, YAN'AN ZHONGLU, TONGREN LU, ZHENNING LU, YUYUAN LU, JIANGSU LU, XUANHUA LU, ANHUA LU, LIXI LU, XINHUA LU

MEMORIAL FOR THE FIRST CONGRESS OF THE CPC

FUXING PARK

SUN YAT-SEN'S FORMER R[ESIDENCE]

The stores on the smart Huaihai Lu stock all the big names in designer fashion, making it the place to be seen for wealthy, fashion-conscious locals. South of this grand boulevard, however, cars are replaced by bicycles and you can take an unhurried stroll in the shade of the plane trees and admire the elegant villas of the old French Concession. This is the pedestrian district of Xintiandi, an area of recently restored traditional *shikumen* houses, where an array of distinctive modern shops, hip boutiques, art galleries and restaurants has now opened. It is a strange but fascinating place where old Shanghai meets the 21st century.

FRAGRANT CAMPHOR GARDEN   PARK 97

RESTAURANTS

Chang Lang Pavilion
沧浪亭 沧浪亭 (**D** C2)
→ 1465 Fuxing Zhonghlu
Tel. 6437 2222
Daily 7am–10pm
A haunt of the employees of the many consulates in the area. Austere but attractive decoration and excellent, unpretentious food: large bowls of noodle soup come with eel or beef with oyster sauce. Carte ¥15.

People 7 (**D** C1)
→ 805 Julu Lu
Tel. 5404 0707
Daily 11.30am–1am
An original, avant-garde setting for a surprisingly good fusion of Taiwanese, Japanese and continental cuisine. The reasonably-priced lunch set menu lets you taste four courses. After 8 pm the restaurant becomes a lounge; the People Bar next door (there is no sign, look for a spotlight in the pavement) is a magnet for Shanghai's hip set. Carte ¥40. If People 7 is full, **Shintori** next door, at no. 803, is equally fun (tel. 5404 5252).

Fragrant Camphor Garden 香樟花园 (**D** C2)
→ 2 Hengshan Lu
Tel. 6433 4385
Daily 10am–2am
A lively bar-restaurant in a very elegant house in the old French Concession. Soups, salads and pizzas, but also more imaginative dishes too (cod marinated in soya). Good value for money. Carte ¥60.

Yin 音 (**D** D2)
→ 59 Maoming Nanlu
Tel. 5466 5070
Daily noon–2pm, 6–10pm
Soft lighting, polished tables and dark parquet floors in a huge dining room looking onto the shopping mall of the Hotel Jinjiang. Recipes from Shanghai and Japan; wine from all over the world. Carte ¥70.

Le Garçon Chinois
乐家尔松 (**D** C2)
→ Hengshan Lu, pavilion 3
Tel. 6445 7970
Daily 6pm–1am
Nothing's French here but the name of the place. You have a choice between modern Spanish cooking on the first floor and Vietnamese food on the second (complete with waitresses in kimonos). On fine days you can sit in the garden on the terrace. Carte ¥70.

Lei Garden Seafood Restaurant
利苑海鲜酒楼 (**D** D2)
→ 965 Huaihai Zhonghlu
Tel. 6445 3538

BAR

FACE

SHANGHART

Mon-Fri 2.30pm, 5–10pm; Sat-Sun 10am–10pm
The second floor is a perfect vantage point for observing the stylish shoppers on the avenue below, and the numerous advertising billboards on the surrounding rooftops. Cantonese specialties: chicken with coconut milk, shark, whole crabs in spicy sauce. You can also choose dim sum (small steamed dishes) from the 'photo album' menu. Carte ¥80.

Lapis Lazuli
藏珑坊 (**D** C2)
→ *9 Dongping Lu*
Tel. 6473 1021
Daily 11.30am–1.30am
Quiet bar on the ground floor, with a small terrace surrounded by bamboos and houses with lush vegetation. Subdued lighting creates a Zen-like atmosphere on the mezzanine under the roof, decorated almost entirely with wood. International cuisine (sushi, risotto, pasta). Impeccable service. Very reasonably priced lunch menu. Carte ¥70 for lunch, ¥200 for dinner.

Old Shanghai Moon
老夜上海 (**D** D1)
→ *59 Maoming Nanlu*
Tel. 6472 6386 Daily, 24 hrs
The ambience may be

slightly old-fashioned but the opening hours make it popular with even the trendiest night-birds. Daily specials, classic Chinese cuisine and local dishes. Carte ¥100.

TMSK 透明思考 (**D** F1)
→ *1 Taicang Lu, Xintiandi square. Tel. 6326 2227*
Daily 1.30pm–1.30am
This restaurant in the newly fashionable district of Xintiandi can be spotted by its two pillars of brightly colored bricks. The equally striking interior design plays with light and transparency. Attentive service and interesting menu: mixed green salad with croutons, beef with truffles. Carte ¥100.

Park 97 (**D** E2)
→ *2 Gaolan Lu*
Tel. 5283 2208
Daily 11.30am–2.30am
Superb dining room decorated with Art-Deco frescos and lit by a large bay window overlooking Fuxing Park. Innovative Italian and Japanese cooking. Carte ¥200.

BARS, CLUB

FACE 印泰餐饮 (**D** D2)
→ *118 Ruijin Erlu, bldg 4*
Tel. 6466 4328
Daily noon–2am

With a fabulous setting amid the greenery of the Ruijin Guest House (villas decorated in Southeast Asian style), FACE attracts anyone eager to escape the sometimes infernal rhythm of the city. Take your vodka martini on the lawn or the terrace, or sit inside the tasteful colonial-style house, and relax. Happy hour 5–8pm.

Home Bar (**D** D2)
→ *18 Gaolan Lu*
Tel. 5382 0373
Daily 8pm–2am
One of Shanghai's first gay bars. Live shows, with performers turning the bar in the middle of the room into a stage.

California Club
加里福尼亚俱乐部 (**D** E2)
→ *2 Gaolan Lu*
Tel. 5383 2208
Daily 9pm–2.30am
One of the city's trendiest and most upscale nightclubs, with a varied (and loud) music program (acid jazz, funk, house, etc.) International DJs at the weekend.

ART GALLERIES, SHOPPING

ShanghART 香格纳画廊 (**D** E2)
→ *220 Gaolan Lu*
Tel. 6359 3923

Daily 9.30am–9pm
One of Shanghai's most renowned showcases for contemporary Chinese art, founded by Lorenz Hebling, a Swiss who has lived in China for almost 20 years.

Flower market
法国租界花市场 (**D** D2)
→ *225 Shanxi Nanlu*
Daily 9am–9pm
The old greyhound track (Bouvier, 1928) is now taken over by a wonderful selection of orchids.

Shanghai Xiangyang clothing gifts market
(**D** D-C2)
→ *999 Huaihai Zhonghlu*
Daily 9am–8.30pm
Large colorful market selling remainders: clothes, jewelry, watches, souvenirs, etc.

Madame Mao's Dowry
毛太设计 (**D** B2)
→ *70 Fuxing Xilu*
Tel. 6437 1255
Daily 10am–7pm
You'll find here a wide and interesting range of Mao-era memorabilia, vintage clothes, furniture and Chinese decorative items.

Unique Hill Gallery
奇岗草堂 (**D** A4)
→ *907 Tianyaoqiao Lu, apt 301*
Tel. 130 0325 7861 (by appt)
A collection of advertising posters from the interwar period, assembled by its keen owner over decades.

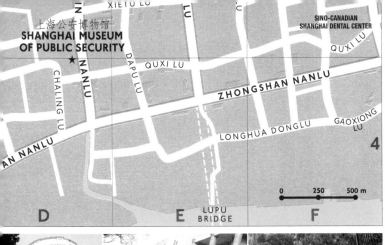

M OF ARTS & CRAFTS

SHANGHAI LIBRARY

SONG QINGLING'S RESIDENCE

he oval ballroom, with
nt Art Deco bas-reliefs
d out by the sunlight
ng through the
m glass roof.

**anghai Museum
blic Security (D** D4)
→ Ruijin Nanlu
402 5172
9am–4.30pm
ntrance has bas-reliefs
g tribute to the
police force from its
ians of law and order.
e, the museum traces
nly the history of the
on in 1854 but also its
increase in resources.
r is devoted to Old
ghai. On the way out,
reens show local
policemen and

congratulation messages
from foreign colleagues!

★ **Shanghai Museum
of Arts & Crafts (D** C2)
→ 79 Fenyang Lu
Tel. 6431 1431
Daily 9am–4pm
The neoclassical house
(1905) belonging to a city
councillor in the French
Concession became the
first mayor of Shanghai's
residence in 1950. The
upper stories now provide
workshop space for
craftsmen, while the ground
floor is a shop-exhibition
space for their work.

★ **Shanghai Library (D** B2)
→ 1555 Huaihai Zhonglu
Tel. 6445 5555
Daily 9am–8.30pm

The city's public library
(1996) is one of the biggest
and most modern in Asia,
with a state-of-the-art
auditorium, reading rooms
and facilities for concerts,
movies and exhibitions.

★ **Soong Ching Ling's
Residence (D** A3)
→ 1843 Huaihai Zhonglu
Tel. 6437 6268
Daily 9am–4.30pm
Sun Yat-sen's widow lived
here from 1948 to 1963, and
Mao Zedong visited her in
1961. While her sisters were
avid for power and money –
the elder one married the
head of the Guomindang,
Chiang Kai-shek, and the
younger one the banker
H.H. Kung (a descendant of

Confucius) – Soong Ching
Ling (1893–1981) founded
the China League for Civil
Rights in 1932 and threw in
her lot with the Communists.

★ **Ruijin
Guest House (D** D2)
→ 118 Ruijin Erlu
The villas spread out over
this large park were built in
the 1920s and 1930s, and
served to house guests of
the Communist Party until
1979. They are now open to
the public and their leafy
grounds are often used by
wedding parties in Western
clothes as a backdrop for
their photo sessions. Many
of the plants are rare, and
their foliage provides refuge
for a host of songbirds.

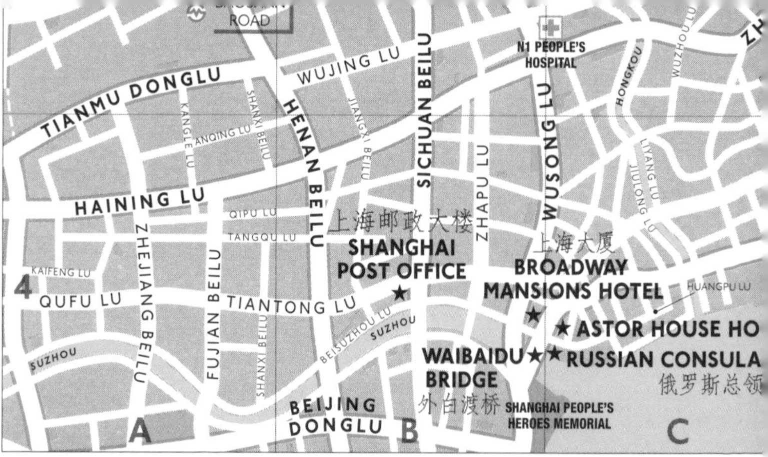

Map (top portion)

TIANMU DONGLU

WUJING LU

HENAN BEILU

SICHUAN BEILU

N1 PEOPLE'S HOSPITAL

WUSONG LU

HONGKOU

WUZHOUJIU

ZH

HAINING LU

ZHEJIANG BEILU

KANGLE LU

ANDING LU

SHANXI BEILU

JIANGXI BEILU

ZHAPU LU

HUANGPU LU

JIULONG LU

QIPU LU

TANGOU LU

上海邮政大楼
SHANGHAI POST OFFICE ★

上海大厦
BROADWAY MANSIONS HOTEL

HUANGPU LU

4 QUFU LU

KAIFENG LU

SUZHOU

FUJIAN BEILU

SHANXI LU

TIANTONG LU

BEISUZHOU LU

SUZHOU

★ **ASTOR HOUSE HO**

★★ **RUSSIAN CONSULA**

俄罗斯总领

BEIJING DONGLU

WAIBAIDU ★★ **BRIDGE**
外白渡桥 SHANGHAI PEOPLE'S HEROES MEMORIAL

A   B   C

DUOLUN LU

LU XUN PARK

★ **Waibaidu Bridge** (**E** B4)
Although recently paired with a much more imposing structure, the Waibaidu Bridge (1907), at the confluence of the Suzhou and the Huangpu, nevertheless still offers fine views of the Pudong skyscrapers and the barges going up the river. When illuminated at night, its metal forms take on a pretty gold tinge.

★ **Russian Consulate** (**E** C4)
→ 20 Huangpu Lu
The white, red and blue flag flying from a high mast and the lone Russian soldier standing guard at one end

of Waidaibu Bridge herald the only consulate that wasn't closed down when the Communists came to power in 1949. When the Chinese broke off relations with their Soviet comrades in 1960, the building was turned into a sailors' club, but it reverted to its former function in 1987.

★ **Broadway Mansions Hotel** (**E** B4)
→ 20 Beisuzhou Lu
This brick hotel, in the form of an elongated X (Palmer & Turner and Flint, 1934), embodies the guiding principles of the Chicago School: height and sobriety. In World War Two the

Japanese occupying forces took advantage of its strategic position at the far end of the Bund by making it their headquarters.

★ **Astor House Hotel** (**E** C4)
→ 15 Huangpu Lu
Tel. 6324 6388
One of the city's oldest hotels – and the most prestigious until the opening of the Peace Hotel in 1929 – the Astor House (1860, enlarged in 1910) was built by two influential Jewish families, the Kadoorie and the Ezra. In the 1990s the Victorian-style ballroom was used as the trading room of the

Shanghai Stock Excha

★ **Shanghai Post Office** (**E** B4)
→ 250 Beisuzhou Lu
The former central pos office (1924) of the International Settleme now serves the whole Its long, low façade overlooking the Suzho River is set off by an elegant colonnade and impressive neoclassic clock tower.

★ **Duolun Lu** (**E** B2)
This street, with its pre restored houses and a American church, is cl to cars so it has been over by bicycles and neighbors chatting on

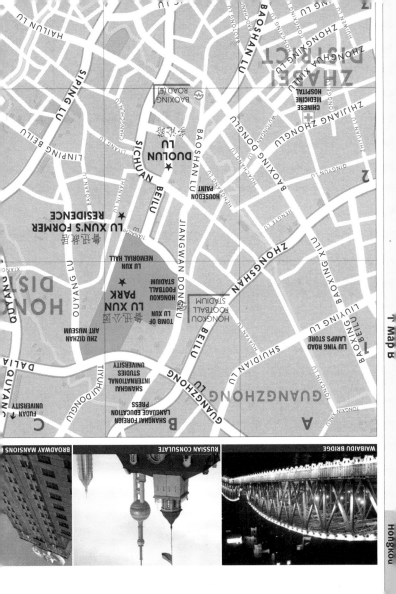

Map B

WAIBAIDU BRIDGE

RUSSIAN CONSULATE

BROADWAY MANSIONS

The parade of architectural treasures along the Bund extends from the north bank of the Suzhou to the metal Waibaidu Bridge. However, the highlight of the Hongkou district is Sichuan Beilu, a bustling shopping street that leads north to the popular Lu Xun Park, named after a famous writer who lived in a *lilong* in this neighborhood. Beyond the park, student life becomes increasingly evident, as the city's most prestigious center of learning, the Fudan University, lies close by. On Dongdaming Lu, which runs alongside the Huangpu, the warehouses are being taken over by art galleries and there are plans to install new tourist attractions in the docks.

F HAPPINESS RESTAURANT

SEAGULL HOTEL TE

RESTAURANTS

Le Tao Tao
乐陶陶 (**E** C1)
→ 427 Tiyuhui Donglu
Tel. 6554 4727
Daily 10am–10pm
Students get a 15 percent discount so, naturally, they form a substantial part of the clientele of this small restaurant. The mushroom soup is highly recommended. Carte ¥15.

F Happiness Restaurant
大名店 (**E** C4)
→ 713 Dongdaming Lu
Tel. 6595 0990
Daily 9.30am–10pm
Near the galleries on Dongdaming Lu, a meeting place for artists. The novelist Mian Mian, the movie director Zhang Yuan, the poet Li Xing and other celebrities have all left their signature on the stairwell. Spicy dishes from Hunan and Sichuan, are served in beautiful bowls. The chilli content can be adjusted to your personal taste. Carte ¥30.

Shanghai Renjia
上海人家 (**E** B2)
→ 50 Tianaizhi Lu
Tel. 5696 7979
Daily 11am–2pm, 5–9pm
Part of the 'Shanghai Family' chain, which has carved a niche in the city by concentrating on local specialties: tofu coated with caramel, seafood with orange, sweet stuffed lotus root, etc. Carte ¥40.

Shanghai Maiziwang Hotel上海麦子王饭店 (**E** C4)
→ 809 Dongdaming Lu
Tel. 6595 3683
Daily 11am–2pm, 5–10pm
Watch your dishes being prepared through the windows that separate the kitchen and the dining room of the restaurant. Shellfish and specialties from northern China (including a wide range of ravioli). Carte ¥50.

Sightseeing Riverbank Restaurant
海鸥饭店滨江观景餐厅 (**E** C4)
→ 60 Huangpu Lu
Tel. 6356 4280
Daily 11am–11pm
The tables are set inside the sampans deposited on the terrace of the five-star Shanghai Seagull Hotel, situated at the confluence of the Huangpu and Suzhou Creek. Recipes from Shanghai, Jiangsu and Taiwan, with many fish and seafood dishes. Great view of the Huangpu. Carte ¥50.

REHOUSE

HONGKOU FOOTBALL STADIUM

SHANGHAI SHANG WU ZHONG XING

BARS

Tsingtao Beer Pub
青岛啤酒吧 **(E** B2)
→ *2365 Sichuan Beilu*
Tel. 5696 5655
Daily 10am–2am
The famous Tsingtao beer is the main attraction here: no less than seven types of beer brewed by the Tsingtao company are served in bottles or on draft. Entertainment every night from 8.30pm to 11pm: concert (Mon-Tue, Thu-Fri) or karaoke (Wed, Sat-Sun).

Sunflower English Club 太阳花英语村
(E B1)
→ *Lu Xun Park*
Tel. 6587 3763
Daily 9.30am–9.30pm
This café in Lu Xun Park does its best to conjure up a typically English atmosphere: a dark brick fireplace, Victorian-style wallpaper, a clock chiming the hours and terraces overflowing with plants. Beers, whiskies, cocktails.

Reading Room Café
阅读坊咖啡馆 **(E** B2)
→ *195 Duolun Lu*
Tel. 5696 2663
Mon-Fri 1pm–midnight;
Fri-Sun noon–midnight
The stove in the entrance manages to heat the whole interior in winter. You can browse in the library running along an entire wall before climbing the narrow staircase leading to the mezzanine, the balcony and the loft. Also on offer: a large selection of flower teas, coffee and French wines.

ART GALLERIES, SHOPPING

Holiday Mall
弘基假日广场 **(E** B4)
→ *318 Tiantong Lu*
Daily 9am–9.30pm
An American-style shopping mall spread over two levels. Very stylish design, with light pouring through a glass roof. Fashionable clothes at very reasonable prices.

Center of Tea from Home and Abroad
(E C4)
→ *137-147 Dongdaming Lu*
Daily 9am–9pm
Selecting a good tea requires as much skill as choosing a good wine, but it is a dying art and in 2002 the local authorities launched a three-year program to train specialist tea-makers. Beginners can try over 1,000 types of tea on offer. Use mineral water for the best results.

Dongdaming Lu
东大名路 **(E** C4)
→ *713 Dongdaming Lu*
Old warehouses by the docks, now converted into art galleries.

DDM Warehouse
东大名仓库
→ *Tel. 3501 3212*
Tue-Sun 10.30am–6pm;
www.ddmwarehouse.cn
Paintings and installations by foreign artists in an enormous hangar.

Aura Gallery
亦安艺术
→ *Tel. 6595 0901*
Daily 10am–6pm;
www.aura-art.com
William Zhang's gallery opened in 2000 to promote young Chinese artists and photographers. Housed in a 1925 warehouse, the gallery offers a beautiful view of the docks.

Zhu Qizhan Art Museum
朱屺瞻艺术中心 **(E** C1)
→ *580 Ouyang Lu*
Tel. 5666 1967
Daily 10am–5pm
In the entrance to the museum devoted to the painter Zhu Qizhan (1892–1996), there is this small gallery with works by contemporary Chinese painters and sculptors.

Shanghai Shang Wu Zhong Xing
上海商务中心 **(E** C1)
→ *800 Quyang Lu*
Tel. 6553 8682
Daily 9.30am–5.30pm
Toward the suburbs, a shopping mall with bargain prices: food, hi-fi, furniture.

Lamp market
上海灯具城 **(E** A1)
→ *125 Liuying Lu*
Daily 9am–6pm
A large concrete gate, unveiled in 2003, announces the 'City of Lights': garish neon, standard lamps, advertising billboards in Chinese characters, and the whole gamut of electrical fixtures.

SPORT

Hongkou Football Stadium
虹口足球场 **(E** B1)
→ *444 Jiangwan Donglu*
Tel. 6540 0009
This stadium has been the home ground for Shenhua Football Club (one of Shanghai's top two soccer teams) since 1999 and it regularly attracts up to 35,000 spectators.

HONGKOU DISTRICT
CENTRAL HOSPITAL

DISTRICT

INTERNATIONAL
PASSENGER
TERMINAL

YANGSHUPU LU

WATER
PURIFICATION ★
PLANT

Map F →

4

HUANGPU

D   E   F

0   250   500 m

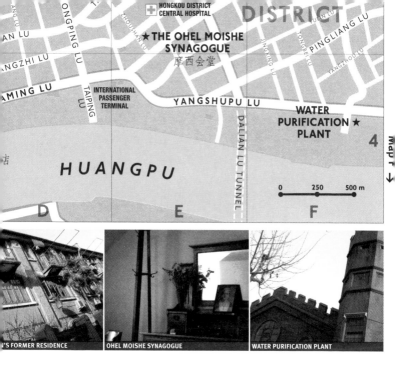

I'S FORMER RESIDENCE   OHEL MOISHE SYNAGOGUE   WATER PURIFICATION PLANT

alk. In the 1920s it
ome to members of
eague of Leftist Writers,
ncluded Lu Xun (its
er), Ye Shentao and
Mojuo; all three are
nemorated by statues.

Xun Park (**E** B1)
88 Sichuan Beilu
6am–6pm
arge park in northern
y all day round, with
ls practising tai chi in
orning, fishermen
g away the hours
r the weeping willows
ouples talking by the
us shores of the lake.
amed after the father
dern Chinese

literature, Lu Xun
(1881–1936), whose tomb,
guarded by a bronze statue,
lies within the grounds.
★ Lu Xun's Former
Residence (E B2)
→ 132 Shanyin Lu
Tel. 5666 2608
Daily 9am–4pm
Lu Xun lived in this small
street backing on a lilong
from 1933 until his death.
Take a guided tour of his
modest living quarters.
The apartment next door
contains a library devoted
to this pioneer of vernacular
Chinese literature, whose
most famous works are
Diary of A Madman and
The True Story of Ah Q.

★ Ohel Moishe
Synagogue (E E3)
→ 62 Changyang Lu
Tel. 6541 5008
Daily 9am–4pm
This synagogue was built
in 1927 by Shanghai's
Ashkenazi community. The
first Jews to settle in the city
came from Iraq via India, in
the footsteps of the British.
The Russian Revolution in
October 1917 led to a
further influx of Jews, and
their numbers were swelled
still further, after 1938, by
Jews from Central Europe
fleeing Nazi persecution;
between 1937 and 1939
20,000 Jews settled in
Shanghai, where no

entrance permit was
required. In 1941, when
the city was occupied by
the Japanese, a Jewish
ghetto was built in this
neighborhood.
★ Water purification
plant (E F4)
→ 600 Yangshupu Lu
This vast complex was
built in 1881 by the British
as a pastiche of a castle,
complete with crenellated
walls and corner towers.
The plant was enhanced by
gardens and tennis courts,
and it contained equipment
that was extremely modern
in its day. There is a good
view of the building from
the Huangpu River.

LUJIAZUI DEVELOPMENT SHOWROOM

SHANGHAI STOCK EXCHANGE

★ Oriental Pearl TV Tower (F A1)

→ *1 Shiji Dadao*
Tel. 5879 1888
Daily 8.30am–9.30pm

The Orient Pearl (1994), strategically located on a bend in the Huangpu, has become the symbol of the city of Shanghai. You, too, will be taken by it if you arrive from the airport by night as it is a striking building to emerge from the skyline. This arrangement of spheres and shafts, resembling a rocket waiting for liftoff (or, for the Chinese, two dragons playing with a pearl) soars 1,535 feet above the ground. The elevator propels visitors to an altitude of 1,150 feet in only a few seconds, providing them with a dizzying view of the urban sprawl on both sides of the Huangpu.

★ Shanghai Municipal History Museum (F A1)

→ *Oriental Pearl TV Tower*
1 Shiji Dadao. Tel. 5879 3003
Daily 9am–9pm

Photos hung in the entrance of Shanghai's old concessions and streets swarming with rickshaws. This museum at the bottom of the TV Tower goes on to tell the history of the city via a series of animated reconstructions, which include various types of exhibits, old Chinese shops, British gunboats opening up the city to the opium trade in 1843, etc. Also on display are several well-made models – of the Bund, of the Hardoon garden.

★ Shanghai Ocean Aquarium (F A1)

→ *1388 Lujiazui Ring Road*
Tel. 5877 9988
Daily 9am–9pm

This rather ordinary-looking building houses a huge space devoted to the world under the sea. One tank with sharks and rays is crossed by a long transparent tunnel, while others display an array of jellyfish or a reconstruction of a coral reef. In all, over 10,000 specimens from 3,000 different specie

★ Riverbank Boulevard (F A1-A2)

→ *Binjiang Dadao*
Daily 7am–10.30pm

The 'New Bund' prome running parallel to the Bund, has been create on the east shore of th river – so close that yo hear the water lapping When the sun goes do the Bund, only the ou of its monumental bui are visible – this is de the best spot for viewi the famous quay.

★ Jinmao Tower (F B

→ *88 Shiji Dadao*
Tel. 6541 5008

Built in 1998, this is a architectural masterpi

↓ Map E

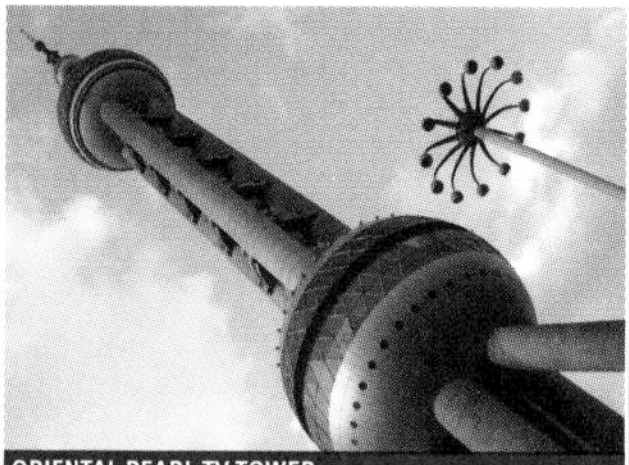

PUDONG
NEW DISTRICT

LAOS...

ZHANGYANG LU

TIMES SQUARE

SHANGHAI INTERNATIONAL BUSINESS CITY

PUCHENG LU

SHANGCHENG LU

LAOSHAN XILU

LAOSHAN DONGLU

DONGCHANG LU

DONGCHANG ROAD

PUMIN LU

DONGTAI LU

YINCHENG NANLU

QIXIA LU

上海证券交易所

SHANGHAI STOCK EXCHANGE

HUAYUANSHIQIAO LU

香格里拉

JINMAO TOWER

YINCHENG DONGLU

YINCHENG ZHONGLU

YINCHENG DADAO

FUCHENG LU

BINJIANG DADAO

ZHAOYUAN LU

ORIENT HOSPITAL

陆家嘴开发开放陈列馆

LUJIAZUI DEVELOPMENT SHOWROOM

LUJIAZUI GREEN LAND

滨江大道

RIVERBANK BOULEVARD

JIMO LU

PUDONG

CHANGYI LU

DALIAN LU TUNNEL

上海东方明珠广播电视塔

ORIENTAL PEARL TV TOWER

海洋世界水族馆

SHANGHAI OCEAN AQUARIUM

LUJIAZUI XILU

LUJIAZUI

SUPER BRAND MALL

上海历史陈列馆

SHANGHAI MUNICIPAL HISTORY MUSEUM

BUND TUNNEL

FUXING DONGLU TUNNEL

FUXING DONGLU

BAIDI LU

LAOTAIPING LONG

C

B

A

1

2

ORIENTAL PEARL TV TOWER

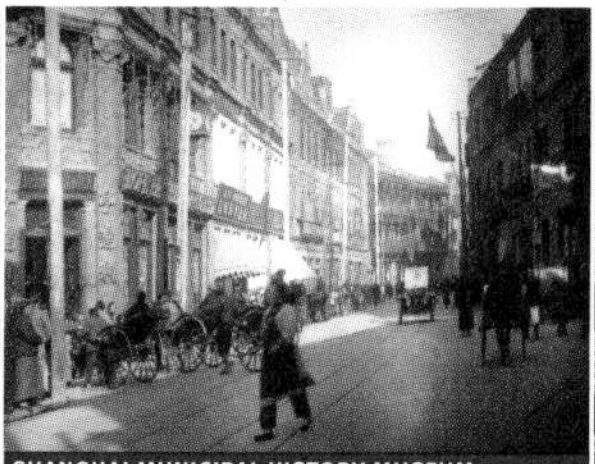

SHANGHAI MUNICIPAL HISTORY MUSEUM

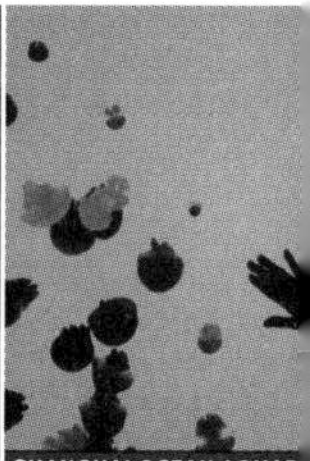

SHANGHAI OCEAN AQUAR

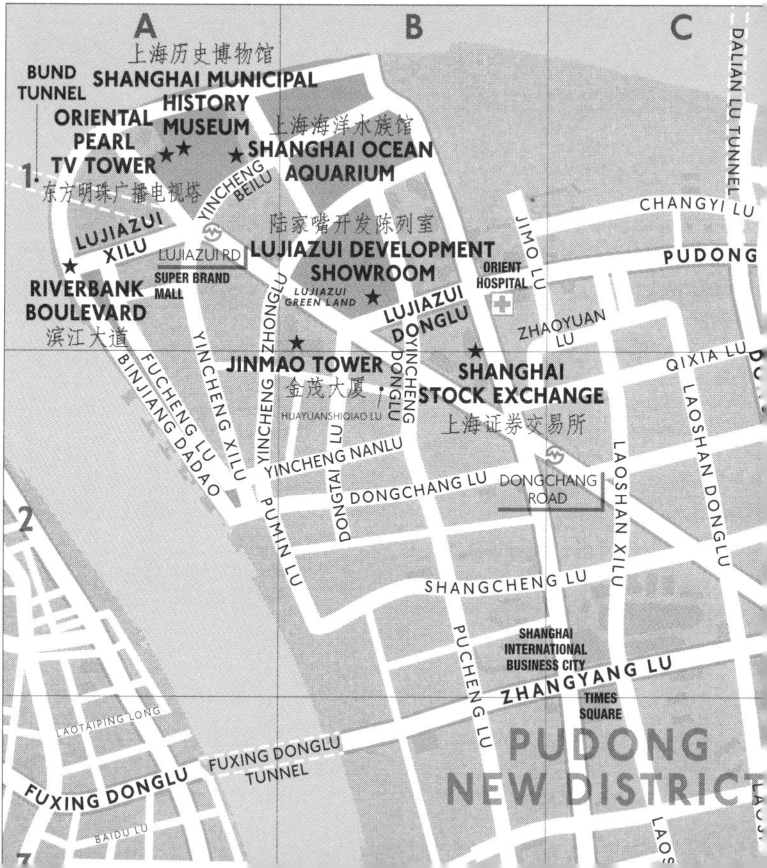

Pudong

F

Pudong ('east of the river') has been in the grips of a development boom since the early 1990s. The planning project for this area was to attract new investment and make Shanghai a major player on the world stage. This is now a reality: in a mere ten years a new city has sprung up, extending over 185 square miles, and most of Shanghai's financial and trading activities will be concentrated here in the future. Pudong boasts the world's first magnetic train and a multimedia scientific theme park. But environmental concerns have not been overlooked: thousands of trees have been planted along its central axis, Shiji Dadao ('boulevard of the century'), which leads to an enormous park.

DONG SHANGHAI DA JIUDIAN CAFÉ RAMA

RESTAURANTS

Dong Shanghai Da Jiudian
东上海大酒店 (**F** C3)
→ *1455 Pudong Nanlu*
Tel. 5887 9698 Daily
11.30am–1.30pm, 5–9pm
Handpick your own fish or shellfish from one of the many aquariums in the entrance. On the first floor a young kitchen boy prepares the garlic bread that accompanies the dishes. Carte ¥60.

Halong Bay 夏龙湾 (**F** B1)
→ *15 Lujiazui Donglu*
Tel. 5877 1231
Daily 10am–10pm
Experience elaborate Vietnamese cooking in the attractively designed bright, contemporary house in the Lujiazui Park. Carte ¥80.

Art 50 (**F** C1)
→ *728 Fushan Lu*
Tel. 5036 6666
Daily 6–10pm
A revolving restaurant on the 50th floor of the Novotel Atlantis, 870 feet from the ground. It turns a full circle in 90 minutes to provide stunning views of Pudong. The cuisine is an unusual fusion of East and West: consommé of *bouillabaisse* with wonton (fried ravioli), stuffed with lobster. Carte ¥180.

Grand Hyatt
金茂凯悦大酒店 (**F** B1)
→ *Jianmao Tower*
88 Century Boulevard
Tel. 5049 1234
The Grand Hyatt serves Shanghai's classiest hotel food. There are six restaurants representing several of the world's great culinary traditions. Among them is: **Grand Café**
→ *Daily, 24hrs*
On the 54th floor: a huge international buffet with sandwiches and light meals. Carte ¥100.

BARS, CAFÉS

Century Coffee
世纪咖啡 (**F** F4)
→ *1001 Jinxiu Lu*
Tel. 5033 1758
Daily 9.30am–midnight
For those who fancy an iced tea, a chocolate milkshake or a snack on the bank of the big lake in Century Park. The interior is cooled by a fountain, while there is a tranquil, shady terrace outdoors.

Café Rama
咖啡蓝玛 (**F** B2)
→ *211 Shiji Dadao*
Tel. 5878 0967
Mon–Fri 8am–7pm
This bar in the futuristic foyer of the Shanghai Information Tower, popular with stockbrokers taking a

9

BUND SIGHTSEEING TUNNEL

YIBO GALLERY

break from their work. It also stocks a good selection of newspapers.

Starbucks 星巴克 (**F** A1)
→ *Fu Du Duan, Binjiang Dadao. Tel. 5878 1332 Daily 9.30am–11pm*
You may not like the invasive Starbucks but the location here is perfect, with a fantastic terrace overlooking the Huangpu.

B.A.T.S. 蝙蝠娱乐中心 (**F** A1)
→ *33 Fucheng Lu Tel. 6882 8888 Daily 6pm–2am (3am Fri-Sun). Live music Tue-Sun 9.30pm–1am*
The 'Bar at the Shangri-La', tucked in the basement of the eponymous hotel, has all the trappings of a Western saloon: country or rock music, a wooden floor, rustic furnishings, a dartboard, a barber's chair and barrels as decoration. Wide range of (expensive) beers. A fun place for a good night out. Live music daily (except Sun) 9.30pm–1am.

Jinmao Tower 金茂大厦 (**F** B1)
→ *88 Shiji Dadao*

Piano bar
→ *Mon-Fri 5pm–1am; Sat-Sun 2pm–1am*
The Grand Hyatt Hotel occupies the last 34 stories of the Jinmao Tower. In this lounge-bar,

on the 53rd floor, jazz singers, accompanied by a pianist, perform every night. Wide range of whiskies and cocktails, and a selection of cigars. Spectacular views over the Bund.

Cloud 9
→ *Mon-Fri 6pm–2am; Sat-Sun 11am–2am*
Floating in Heaven. The highest bar in the world, on the tower's 87th floor, designed around a series of striking stainless-steel pillars. The lighting is minimal, thereby enhancing the 360° view of the city lights at night. Wine by the glass, every liquor imaginable and delicious tapas. Very hip, and patronized mainly by Chinese. On the 88th floor is Sky Lounge, favored by expats and travelers.

ATTRACTIONS

Bund Tunnel 外滩观光隧道 (**F** A1)
→ *May-Oct: daily 8am–10.30pm (10pm Nov-April)*
A tunnel with psychedelic lighting effects, linking the Bund with the futuristic Pudong. It plunges under the Huangpu, in front of the Peace Hotel, and re-emerges at the foot of the Pearl Tower.

Shanghai Natural Wild-Insect Kingdom 上海大自然野 (**F** A1)
→ *1 Fenghe Lu Tel. 5840 6950 Daily 9am–5pm (5.30pm in winter)*
The world of insects and reptiles, for children and adults alike: cross-section of an ants' colony, a glasshouse for butterflies, a vivarium for snakes and crocodiles dozing by a pool. You can catch your own goldfish on leaving!

Shanghai Science & Technology Museum 上海科技馆 (**F** E4)
→ *2000 Shiji Dadao Tel. 8854 2000 Tue-Sun 9am–5pm*
Two auditoria equipped with IMAX technology, as for the museum, but without the smoke and water effects!

Imax 3D
Very realistic, three-dimensional effects seen through special glasses.

Imax Dome
A screen with a diameter of 100 feet and a state-of-the-art sound system.

Rental of pedal boats (**F** E4)
→ *Jinxiu Lu Daily 8.30am–4pm*
Explore the Zhangjia canal (the cleanest in the city) from the lake in Century Park to the Huangpu.

SHOPPING, ART GALLERY

Super Brand Mall 正博大广场 (**F** A1)
→ *168 Lujiazui Xilu Tel. 6887 7888 Daily 10am–10pm*
A fleet of colorful buses drops customers in front of China's biggest shopping mall (2002). A supermarket in the basement and 12 floors of stores of all kinds, from car show-rooms to antique dealers.

Yibo Gallery 艺博画廊 (**F** B2)
→ *198 Huayuanshiqiao Lu Tel. 5888 0111 Mon-Sat 10am–7.30pm*
This gallery in front of the Jinmao Tower was opened shortly after the skyscraper. The contemporary Chinese art exhibitions change every two months: photos, oil paintings, sculpture. All the artists leave their mark by signing the wall.

Precinct of Shanghai Science & Technology Museum Subway Station (**F** E4)
→ *2000 Shiji Dadao Sat-Sun: sunrise–sunset*
This is taken over at weekends by kite-fliers. If you want to join in, you can buy kites here, from simple paper butterflies to veritable collectors' items.

PUDIAN LU

SHANGHAI SCIENCE & TECHNOLOGY MUSEUM

HEHUAN LU

YINGSHUN LU

★ **SHANGHAI SCIENCE & TECHNOLOGY MUSEUM**
上海科技馆

YANGGAO NANLU

ZHANGJIA

JINXIU LU

CENTURY PARK
世纪公园 ★

JINGTIAN LAKE

4

JINXIU LU

HUAMU LU

0   250   500 m

D   E   F

AI SCIENCE & TECHNOLOGY MUSEUM

CENTURY PARK

kyscraper spans ories (eight being the associated with luck na). A steel filigree s the glass structure, it a golden hue at t. The interior is tuously decorated: :olored metal plaques entrance, antiques ery floor. There is a nous 30-story atrium heart of the Grand Hotel, which occupies tire top section of yscraper.

jiazui Development vroom (F B1)
➔ .ujiazui Donglu
°87 9964
3.30am–6pm
egant brick mansion

(1917), centered on a huge courtyard. The first few rooms have conserved their traditional decoration, while the rooms overlooking the courtyard reflect the amazing expansion of the Lujiazui neighborhood, showing development studies and futuristic plans drawn up in the 1990s.

★ **Shanghai Stock Exchange (F** B1-2)
➔ 528 Pudong Nanlu
Tel. 6880 8888
The Stock Exchange, the symbol of Shanghai's financial aspirations, was recently transferred to this arch surrounded by office blocks. In the 1930s Shanghai was the world's

third largest trading center, and it is now intent on recovering the ground lost to its biggest Asian rivals – Tokyo and Hong Kong.

★ **Shanghai Science and Technology Museum (F** E4)
➔ 2000 Shiji Dadao
Tel. 6862 2000
Daily 9am–5pm
A huge crescent moon protecting a geodesic dome provides the setting for the largest science museum in China, which opened in 2001. 'Journey to the Center of the Earth' (geology), 'Light of Wisdom' (physical and chemical phenomena, and mathematical laws), 'Cradle of the Designers'

(computer-assisted creation), 'The Whole Spectrum of Life' (glasshouse presenting tropical fauna and flora) and interactive animation.

★ **Century Park (F** F4)
➔ 1001 Jinxiu Lu
Daily 7am–5pm
Go down the walkway adorned with lamps in the form of birds in flight: the panoramic view of the Shiji Gongyuan, the biggest green space in Shanghai (345 acres), is spectacular. The sky here is studded with hundreds of kites at the weekend. Tandems for hire, swings and pedal boats on the Jingtian Lake – the perfect spot for a picnic.

ACCESS TO AIRPORTS

Pudong Int. Airport
Shanghai Maglev
→ *The world's first magnetic levitation train, traveling at up to 267mph! From Longyang subway: 8-minute trip.*
Bus
→ *Line 1 (Hongqiao Airport)*
→ *Line 2 (Jingan Temple)*
→ *Line 3 (Xujiahui)*
For all 3 lines: daily 7.20am–midnight; every 30 mins.
→ *Line 4 (Lu Xun Park)*
Daily 7.20am–11pm; every 40 mins
→ *Line 5 (Shanghai Railway Station) Daily 5.30am–8pm*
Hongqiao Airport
Taxi
→ *20 mins from the center*

PUDONG INTERNATIONAL AIRPORT

PUDONG INTERNATIONAL AIRPORT

TAXI

More than 50,000 taxis crisscross the city, which means they are available at any time and any place.
→ *Minimum fare ¥10 (¥13 from 11pm) valid for first 3 km/1.85 miles, then ¥3 /km or ¥4.8 /mile*

CAR

Car rental
→ *¥500/day with driver*
The driver is compulsory as foreign tourists are not allowed to drive.

TRAIN STATIONS

Shanghai Railway Station (B D2)
→ *Info tel. 6317 9090*
Trains for Beijing, Nanjing, Suzhou, etc.
Shanghai South Railway Station
→ *Subway line 1*
This serves Hangzhou.

BUS STATIONS

Shanghai Sightseeing Bus Center (off map)
→ *666 Tianyaoqiao Lu*
Shanghai Stadium subway. Twenty-five excursion routes.
Long-distance buses (B F2)
→ *Gonghe Lu / Qiujiang Lu*

...e Broadway Mansions, built in 1934, offer splendid views of the quay and the night-time illuminations, along with the barges passing under the Waibaidu Bridge. The 234 rooms are charming and offer all the services of a four-star hotel. From ¥700.
Donghu Hotel
东湖宾馆 **(D** C2)
→ *70 Donghu Lu*
Tel. 6415 8158
A beautiful Art-Deco building surrounded by greenery. Large porch, foyer adorned with wrought iron and sculpted marble, and a lounge with old leather couches. High molded ceilings in the 267 spacious rooms. Ask for a room with a balcony. Restaurant, swimming pool. From ¥720.
Taiyuan Binguan
太原宾馆 **(D** C3)
→ *160 Taiyuan Lu*
Tel. 6471 6688 Reopening in 2007 after renovation works

Managed by the same people as the Ruijin, this fabulous villa is hidden by the old trees on its grounds. Relax on the ground floor in one of the many lounges with marble fireplaces; upstairs, the enormous bedrooms are decorated with period furniture. Breakfast on the terrace. Very quiet. From ¥720.
Hengshan Hotel
衡山宾馆 **(D** B3)
→ *534 Hengshan Lu*
Tel. 6437 7050
www.hotelhengshan.com
A petty corner building (1934) in a busy shopping area, with two large parks nearby. Art-Deco-style bedrooms and suites. Restaurants and bars. ¥730.
Anting Villa (D B3)
→ *46 Anting Lu*
Tel. 6433 1188
In the center of a gorgeous park planted with magnolias and cedars, this is the modern 'Villa of Tranquility',

guarded by two lions. It has 120 cozy rooms, a billiard room and karaoke-disco. From ¥780.
Hengshan Moller Villa
衡山马勒别墅饭店 **(B** D4)
→ *30 Shanxi Nanlu*
Tel. 6247 8881
www.mollervilla.com
An imposing neo-Gothic villa (1936) with a tower on top and kitsch decor in the lobby: a fresco depicting a Bavarian country scene. Plus staircases with carved wood banisters, two-toned parquet floors and an attractive terrace with shady trees. Some of the 45 large rooms have a balcony. ¥800.
Pacific Hotel
金门大酒店 **(B** F3)
→ *108 Nanjing Xilu*
Tel. 6327 6226
Classic 1930s building with very fine views of People's Square that equal those of its more famous neighbor, the Park Hotel. Coffered ceiling in the entrance,

PUDONG AIRPORT

SHANGHAI PUXI PUDONG

BAOSHAN

JIADING

CHANGJIANG (YANGZI)

CHONGMING

NANJING

HONGQIAO
AIRPORT

HANGZHOU

MINHANG

PUDONG
INTERNATIONAL
AIRPORT

NANHUI

ACCESS TO AIRPORTS AND MAIN ROADS

AIRPORTS

www.shanghaiairport.com
Pudong International Airport
→ Info tel. 3848 4500
International flights and a few internal flights.
Hongqiao Airport
→ Info tel. 6268 8899
Internal flights only.

The prices listed refer to a standard double room with bathroom and breakfast included. Rooms are generally equipped with a minibar and a kettle. The charges in the top-class hotels are billed in dollars; you can also pay in yuans, but these will be subject to variations in the exchange rate between the two currencies. It is essential to book ahead in spring and fall. Discounts in low season (Jan-Feb and July-Aug) of 10% or more. Many well-equipped rented apartments are also available; some of these can be rented by the day.

RENTED APARTMENTS

Golden City Garden
金 都 苑 (off map)
→ 1310 Dingxi Lu
Tel. 6231 1841
Spacious apartments (over 1,000 square feet) with parquet floors. Office,
two bathrooms and fully fitted kitchen. Big closets and extra-large beds. ¥580 (¥13,000–16,000 per month). Breakfast is not included.

¥300–700

Chunshenjiang Hotel
春申江宾馆 (**A** C3)
→ 626 Nanjing Donglu
Tel. 6351 5710
This hotel's reception is at the end of a small mall that looks onto the busy Nanjing Donglu. The 76 spotless rooms are spread over three stories. On the other floors: night-club, restaurants and a foot massage parlor. ¥330.
Swan Hotel Shanghai
上海天鹅宾馆 (**E** B2)
→ 2211 Sichuan Beilu
Tel. 5666 5666
Opposite the ponds in Lu Xun Park, this hotel is good value for money: 191 spacious and comfortable
rooms from ¥480.
Metropole Hotel
新城饭店 (**A** E3)
→ 180 Jiangxi Zhonglu
Tel. 6321 3030
The glory days of this hotel may be long gone, but it still has a touch of class, especially in the neoclassical foyer lit by impressive chandeliers. Olde-world atmosphere and standard comforts in the 145 enormous rooms; eight restaurants and bars. From ¥550.
Astor House Hotel
蒲江饭店 (**E** C4)
→ 15 Huangpu Lu
Tel. 6324 6388
www.pujianghotel.com
The city's most luxurious hotel, from 1860 to the 1930s, still has a quaint charm. It has retained its parquet floor (now worn with age), its bright patio and paneled foyer. Its 116 enormous rooms (choose a deluxe one) are sparsely
decorated and the bathrooms are rather antiquated, but the hotel is a ten-minute walk from the Bund – magical in the evening. From ¥580.
YMCA 青年会宾馆 (**D** F1)
→ 123 Xizang Nanlu
Tel. 6326 1040
A youth hostel since 1929. The building, with its striking curved roof, was designed by Lin Jinpei, an American architect of Cantonese origin. The 16 rooms and suitesnow have all the modern comforts of a three-star hotel. Ask one at the back, they're quieter. From ¥685.

¥700–1,000

Broadway Mansions Hotel 上海大厦 (**E** B4)
→ 220 Beisuzhou Lu
Tel. 6324 6260
Although set back from the Bund and its heavy traffic, the large bay windows of

Transportation and hotels in Shanghai

The streets, monuments and places to visit are listed below in alphabetical order. They are followed by a reference such as '**A** E2', of which the first letter in bold refers to one or the six geographical areas presented in the guide.

Streets

Anhua Lu **D** A1
Anqing Lu **E** A4
Anshan Lu **E** E1
Anting Lu **D** B3
Anyuan Lu **B** B3
Aomen Lu **B** B2-C2
Baidu Lu **C** C3-D3, **F** A3
Baihe Lu **A** A3
Bangsongyuan Lu **C** B5-B6
Bao'an Lu **E** C2
Baochang Lu **E** A3
Baoding Lu **E** E3
Baoshan Lu **E** A3-B2
Baotong Lu **E** A3-B3
Baoxing Beilu **E** A1
Baoxing Donglu **E** A2-B2
Baoxing Xilu **E** A1-A2
Beihai Lu **A** B4-C4
Beijing Donglu **A** A2-E2, **E** A4-B4
Beijing Xilu **A** A3, **B** C4-F3
Beisuzhou Lu **A** A2-E1, **B** E3-F3, **E** A4-B4
Benxi Lu **E** F1
Binjiang Dadao **C** D1, **F** A2
Caoxi Beilu **D** A4
Caoyang Lu **B** A3
Chaling Lu **D** D4
Chang'an Lu **B** D2-E3
Changchun Lu **E** B2
Changde Lu **B** B2-C4
Changhua Lu **E** C2-D3
Changle Lu **D** D1-E1
Changliu Lu **F** F3-F4
Changning Lu **B** A3-A4
Changning Xilu **B** A3-A4
Changping Lu **B** C3
Changsha Lu **A** A2-A3
Changshou Lu **B** A3-C2
Changshu Lu **D** C1-C2
Changyi Lu **F** C1-D1
Changzhi Lu **A** F1

Chengdu Beilu **B** E2-E3
Chifeng Lu **E** D1-E1
Chongqing Nanlu **D** E1-E2
Cixi Lu **B** E3
Dajing Lu **C** A2
Dalian Lu **E** D1-E3
Dalian Xilu **E** C1-D1
Daming Lu **A** F1
Damuqiao Lu **D** D3-D4
Danshui Lu **D** E2
Dapu Lu **D** E3-E4
Datian Lu **B** E3
Datong Lu **B** E2-E3
Dianchi Lu **A** E3
Dingxiang Luf E3-F3
Dong Jie **C** C2-C3
Dong'an Lu **D** B3-B4
Dongchang Lu **C** D1, **F** A2-B2
Dongchangzhi Lu **E** C-D4
Dongdaming Lu **E** C4-D4
Dongfang Lu **F** C2-D4
Donghu Lu **D** C2
Dongjiadu Lu **C** C4-D4, **F** A3-A4
Dongjiangyin Jie **C** C4, **F** A4
Dongjiayin Jie **C** B4-C4
Dongping Lu **D** B2-C2
Dongtai Lu **C** A2-A3, **D** F1-F2
Dongxin Lu **B** A2
Dongyuhang Lu **E** C3-E3
Emei Lu **A** F1
Fangbang Zhonglu **C** A2-C2
Fangxie Lu **C** A3, **D** F2
Feihong Lu **E** F2
Fenglin Lu **D** C3-C4
Fengyang Lu **A** A3
Fenyang Lu **D** C2
Fucheng Lu **C** D1, **F** A2
Fucun Lu **B** A1
Fujian Beilu **A** C1-C2, **E**A4
Fujian Nanlu **A** D4, **C** A1
Fujian Zhonglu **A** C2-D4
Fumin Lu **D** C1
Fushan Lu **F** D1-D3

Fushun Lu **E** E1-F1
Fuxin Lu **E** E1
Fuxing Donglu **C** A3-D3, **F** A3
Fuxing Xilu **D** A2-B2
Fuxing Zhonglu **D** E2-F2
Fuyou Lu **C** B1
Fuzhou Lu **A** B4-E3
Gansu Lu **A** B1
Gansu Lu **B** B1
Gao'an Lu **D** B2-B3
Gaolan Lu **D** D2
Gaoxiong Lu **C** A6, **D** F4
Gaoyang Lu **E** D3
Gonghe Lu **B** D2-E2
Gonghe Xinlu **B** E1-E2
Gongping Lu **E** D3-D4
Gongxing Lu **B** F1-2, **E** A3
Guangdong Lu **A** B4-E9
Guangfu Lu **B** D2-E3
Guangqi Lu **C** B2-C2
Guangqi Nanlu **C** B3
Guangxi Beilu **A** B3-C4
Guangyuan Lu **D** A3-B3
Guangyuan Xilu **D** A3
Guangzhong Lu **E** B1
Guizhou Lu **A** B3
Gujia Long **B** B2-B3
Guling Lu **A** A3
Guohuo Lu **C** B5
Guoqing Lu **A** A2, **B** F3
Haifang Lu **B** C3-D3
Hailun Lu **E** C3
Hankou Lu **A** B3-E3
Hanzhong Lu **B** D2-E2
Hehuan Lu **F** F3-F4
Henan Beilu **A** C1-D1, **E** B3-B4
Henan Nanlu **A** E4, **C** B1-B4
Henan Zhonglu **A** D2-E4
Hengbang Lu **E** B2
Hengfeng Beilu **B** D2
Hengfeng Lu **B** D1-D3
Hengshan Lu **D** A3-B3
Hengtong Lu **B** E3-E2
Hengye Lu **E** A2
Hongqiao Lu **D** A4
Hongxing Lu **E** A3

Hongzhen Laolu **E** D2
Houjia Lu **C** B2
Huachang Lu **E** A2-B2
Huachi Lu **B** A1-B1
Huaihai Xilu **D** A3
Huamu Lu **F** E4
Huanghe Lu **A** A3, **B** E-F3
Huangpi Beilu **B** F4, **D** E1
Huangpi Nanlu **D** E1-F2
Huangpu Lu **A** F1, **E** C4
Huanyuanshiqiao Lu **F** B2
Huashan Lu **D** A3-B3
Huayan Lu **E** A1-B1
Huayin Lu **B** C1
Huimin Lu **E** F3
Huining Lu **C** A4-B4, **D** F3
Huiwen Lu **B** F2, **E** A3
Hunan Lu **D** A2-B2
Huoshan Lu **E** F3
Huqiu Lu **A** E1-E2
Hutai Lu **B** D1-E1
Jiangning Lu **B** C2-D4
Jiangpu Lu **E** F1-F2
Jiangsu Lu **B** A4, **D** A1
Jianguo Donglu **D** E2- F2
Jianguo Xilu **D** B3-D3
Jianguo Zhonglu **D** D2-E2
Jiangwan Donglu **E** B1-B2
Jiangxi Beilu **A** D1, **E** B3-4
Jiangxi Nanlu **A** E4
Jiangxi Zhonglu **A** D1-E4
Jiangyin Lu **B** E4
Jiaotong Lu **B** B1-E2
Jiaozhou Lu **B** B3-C3
Jimo Lu **F** B1
Jingxing Lu **E** F3-F4
Jingzhou Lu **E** E3
Jining Lu **E** F3
Jinling Donglu **A** D4-F4, **C** B1, **D** E1-F1
Jinling Xilu **D** E1
Jinxi Lu **E** E1
Jinxiu Lu **F** E4-F4
Jinyuan Lu **B** F2-F3
Jiujiang Lu **A** B3-E3
Jiulong Lu **E** B4-C4

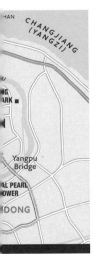

LINE 2 OF THE SUBWAY

Shanghai Public Transportation Card
→ *Price ¥30. Sold in subway stations*
Transferable card, renewable in subway ticket offices.
Valid for subway, buses and taxis.
Subway
Eight lines
→ *¥3–6, depending on the distance*
No special discounts.
Single tickets
Available from automatic machines if you know the cost of the trip; otherwise, buy from the ticket office, stating your destination.
Timetable
→ *Hours vary depending on the line*
Bus and trolley bus
More than 200 lines.
Routes
Maps on sale in bookstores.
Timetable
→ *6am–11pm*
Fares
→ *¥1–4, depending on the distance*
Shanghai Sightseeing Bus Center
→ *Tel. 6426 5555*
Ten tourist bus lines travel round the city (in addition to the excursion lines).
Routes
→ *Departure 666 Tianyaoqiao Lu (Shanghai Stadium)*
Lines numbered from 1 to 10. Destinations include Pudong (line 3) and the main shopping streets (line 10). Line 8 presents *Shanghai by night*.

lying saucer, this hotel provides spectacular views of the Huangpu and the Bocks. From ¥1,950.

Hilton
静安希尔顿饭店 (**D** B1)
→ *250 Huashan Lu*
Tel. 6248 0000
www.hilton.com
The first modern five-star hotel in Shanghai (1987) has 720 rooms with bay windows, spread over 43 floors. Stunning leafy atrium behind the lobby area. From ¥2,360.

The Westin
威斯汀大饭店 (**A** E4)
→ *88 Henan Zhonghlu*
Tel. 6335 1888
www.westin.com
This skyscraper offers expansive views of the Bund. The accent is on modernity, as evident in the contemporary designs of the luminous staircase and the large veranda. Designer furniture in the superb rooms. ¥2,500.

Grand Hyatt
金茂凯悦大酒店 (**F** B1)
→ *88 Shiji Dadao*
Tel. 5049 1234 http://shanghai.grand.hyatt.com
The highest hotel in the world occupies the 34 top floors of the 88-story Jinmao Tower. Stylish contemporary furnishings, Tang pottery and meticulous attention to detail in all the 555 very large rooms. Eye-catching bar at the bottom of the huge atrium, swimming pool, massage parlor, sauna, etc. For a stay in style. ¥2,600.

Portman Ritz Carlton
波特曼丽嘉酒店 (**B** C4)
→ *Shanghai Center, 1376 Nanjing Xilu. Tel. 6279 8888*
www.ritzcarlton.com/hotels/shanghai
At night a jazz band plays in the enormous bar with paneled pillars, which is behind the main entrance, flanked by fountains.

The decoration in this hotel, which opened in 1989 and was refurbished ten years later, is sleek and modern. The 564 rooms are spread over the 26th to 44th floors; there are also several restaurants, bars, lounges, a swimming pool, indoor tennis and squash courts, a sauna, Jacuzzis, etc. From ¥2,800.

88 Xintiandi (**D** E2)
→ *380 Huangpi Nanlu*
Tel. 5383 8833
www.88xintiandi.com
Shanghai's only luxury boutique hotel has 53 rooms decorated in pale hues and dark wood furniture. A definite plus is its location within Xintiandi, a trendy area within the old French concession with a mixture of ancient Chinese architecture and luxury shops, gourmet restaurants and art galleries. Twelve suites, 41 rooms from ¥2,300.

NIGHTIME CRUISE ON THE HUANGPU

CRUISES ON THE HUANGPU

OAT

Shanghai Ferryboats Company

→ Tel. 6326 3560
Boats crossing the Huangpu from some Pupiers. They are now used less often as people mostly use the tunnels.

Boats for Pudong

→ 1 Dong Men Lu
Departs every 20 mins
These disembark near the Jinmao Tower.

CRUISE BOATS

Ticket company (A F4)

→ Yan'an Donglu
Tel. 6329 3246
Daily 9am–10pm

Shanghai Huangpu River Cruise (C C2)

→ Tel. 6374 4461
Departure pier:
119–239 Zhongshan Donglu

East International Tourist Cruise (F A1)

→ Tel. 6860 0016
Departure pier: Oriental Pearl Cruise Dock

Circuits

Suggested types of circuits
Bund-Yanpu Bridge
→ One-hour trip
Bund-Nanpu Bridge-Yanpu Bridge
→ Two-hour trip
Bund-Wusong
→ Three-hour trip
Cruise right up to the mouth of the Yangzi.

International Passenger Terminal (E D4)

→ 100 Yangshupu Lu
Tel. 6595 9529
Departures of shipping lines to Korea and Japan.

and wood as the main decorative element in all the 163 rooms. From ¥800.

Seagull Hotel (E C4)

→ Huangpu Lu
Tel. 6325 1500
www.seagull-hotel.com
Modern hotel with a superb location on the confluence of the Suzhou and the Huangpu. 120 rooms (the best is no.1). From ¥880.

¥1,000–2,000

Shanghai Hotel

上海宾馆 (D B1)
→ 505 Wulumuqi Beilu
Tel. 6248 0088
A large carved panel depicting the Bund presides over the reception of this four-star hotel. Its 543 rooms are particularly popular with Asian guests. Breakfast is served on the veranda. From ¥1,000.

Grosvenor House

贵宾楼 (D D1)
→ Jinjiang Hotel

59 Maoming Nanlu
Tel. 6258 2582
The soothing calm of this 1930s luxury house pervades the 26 magnificent suites, each with its own Art-Deco furniture, loggia and private office. Excellent service. From ¥1,300.

Ruijin Hotel

瑞金宾馆 (D D2)
→ 118 Ruijin Erlu
Tel. 6472 5222
The hotel of the prestigious Ruijin Guest House (see D), is made of five villas decorated in traditional Chinese style, surrounded by greenery yet in the heart of Shanghai; 61 quiet, snug rooms. From ¥1,320.

Peace Hotel

和平饭店 (A E2)
→ 20 Nanjing Donglu
Tel. 6321 6888
www.shanghaipeacehotel.com
The most famous hotel in Shanghai with 380 rooms and suites. The nine deluxe suites are each dedicated to

a country: China, India, Japan, France, Spain, America, Great Britain, Germany and Italy. An attractive terrace overlooks the Huangpu. From ¥1,350.

More than ¥2,000

Sofitel Hyland Shanghai

海仑宾馆 (A C3)
→ 505 Nanjing Donglu
Tel. 6351 5888
www.accorhotels.com
In the middle of the pedestrian section of this street, halfway between the Bund and People's Square. Reception and piano bar on the first floor, 389 colourful rooms. Roof terrace. From ¥1,800.

Novotel Atlantis

海神诺富特大酒店 (F C1)
→ 728 Pudong Dadao
Tel. 5036 6666
www.accorhotels.com
Topped with a revolving restaurant resembling a